Enjoy

Does This Book Make My Butt Look Big?

(And Who Cares Anyway, It's My Butt)

by

Sarah Nilsen

Bloomington, IN Milton Keynes, UK

authorHOUSE®

AuthorHouse™
1663 Liberty Drive, Suite 200
Bloomington, IN 47403
www.authorhouse.com
Phone: 1-800-839-8640

AuthorHouse™ UK Ltd.
500 Avebury Boulevard
Central Milton Keynes, MK9 2BE
www.authorhouse.co.uk
Phone: 08001974150

This book is a work of non-fiction. Unless otherwise noted, the author and the publisher make no explicit guarantees as to the accuracy of the information contained in this book and in some cases, names of people and places have been altered to protect their privacy.

First published by AuthorHouse 4/11/2007

ISBN: 978-1-4343-0408-7 (sc)

Library of Congress Control Number: 2007902642

Printed in the United States of America
Bloomington, Indiana

This book is printed on acid-free paper.

To every woman who has ever
wondered if she is enough.
And to you I say...

Yes you are.

Table of Contents

Introduction

For as long as I can remember, I have wanted to write a book. I just didn't know *what the heck to write about* (and if I couldn't narrow it down to some basic content in the beginning . . . well, you can see why such an undertaking would go into "perma-hold" status).

Then, at the ripe old age of thirty-one, I got the itch to write again—only this time I couldn't ignore it. Chalk it up to my being (a little) older. Or maybe it was the fact that I've done some soul searching and dealt with some of my gremlins (the reality of having dropped out of college before realizing my dream, and the (false) belief that without that degree I wouldn't be seen as "legit" and thus unworthy of the marketplace).

I decided I didn't have to write the great American novel; I could write something different. I could write the *Seinfeld* version, or, as I affectionately refer to it, a book about nothing. At least that's what I thought when I first put pen to paper.

The true stories you are about to enjoy are (mostly) about nothing, but in a good, laugh out loud, cheerfully neurotic way. These are tales of seemingly insignificant, everyday moments where I found clarity that proved to be extraordinary.

These are also the secret confessions of a woman who, though she never clearly states her weight, or anything (hello, this is not meant to be social suicide), does allude to the fact that she struggles with self-esteem, makes silly attempts to fit in, contemplates harebrained schemes to achieve success, and (occasionally) acts on impulses she is *not* proud of. (Does this sound like anyone you know?)

So, here's an opportunity to laugh at me (I mean, laugh *with* me), which I offer in hopes that you, too, will take yourself less seriously. For I've learned that when we can laugh at ourselves, we accept and love ourselves more. And when we embrace the importance of loving ourselves, we can love others more authentically.

And that, ladies (and gentlemen), can heal the world.

Abercrombie & Fitch

Why do I do this to myself?

I had a day off; things were going perfectly fine for me. You know those days when the sun is shining, you make the green lights, your favorite song is on the radio and your hair is über cute since you just got some killer new highlights, plus you're still sporting the blow-out from your stylist. YES! So, what better way to top the day off than a trip to the mall, right? Since I did not need anything in particular (well, truth be told, I did not need anything, period, but when does that ever stop me from shopping?) I decided to parade up and down the mall corridor until something caught my eye.

Now, looking left and right as I walk (who ever shops at those kiosks, anyway?) I am not seeing anything interesting.

Then I hear it. It's that recognizable "thumping" coming from one of the trendy clothing stores. The music is kind of catchy . . . I like it . . . I like it. Why not swing in to see if there are any "must haves"?

I am sorry, have I just walked into the children's department? There is no way on God's green earth that these clothes were made for adults. I better make my way to the back of the store where the women's section is. Nope. Why are these tiny little seventeen-year-old sales people looking at me funny? Is there something on my face? Do I have toilet paper stuck to the bottom of my shoe?

Then it hits me like a ton of bricks. This *is* the adult section. These *are* women's clothes! What? I immediately look for the stretchy tops that I think I can get by with. I need something elastic, and I see a table of carefully folded tank tops across the store. Can I make it over there discreetly? I can feel the sales gals eyeballing me, surely thinking it is a little odd that someone be Christmas shopping in July (because obviously I, personally, could not be looking to fit into anything they can offer).

At last. Elastic. Tank tops. No sleeves to worry about creating that ever-desirable human sausage look. No zippers to try to fasten, as if I am Inspector #12, overseeing the "durability test" at the manufacturer's request. No buttons to remind me that I have all kinds of proportion issues when it comes to my ever-present chest. Just friendly "I look good on everyone" elastic tank tops.

I grab the one from the middle of the pile. What a nice shade of blue. I just *know* it will accentuate my eyes. Perfect. I do the hold-it-up-to your-torso-to-see-if-it-will-fit test. Uh, not quite. This particular top, though stretchy cotton and spandex, would likely disintegrate into teeny-tiny cotton and spandex dust flakes if I tried to pull it over my head. It is obviously an XXS, and I need a Medium. I check the size.

Somebody check my pulse, please. Am I still here? Did I die and enter the Barbie Dream Mall? Last time I checked, "L" stood for Large. That is obviously not the case at this particular store. "L" must stand for "Little" here. Perhaps I should dig for the "S," which might very well stand for "Sexy," or "Supergirl," or something cute like that. Just as I am coming to grips with the fact that I am out of my element with these new sizing terms, a perky little (and I do mean little) sales girl approaches to my left, nine o'clock.

"Hello, Ma'am, can I help you find something?"

Okay, hold it right there. Did I just get ma'amed? Did this pint-sized, prepubescent little tramp just call me Ma'am? When did I become a Ma'am? (Did she see me in the parking lot? I knew I should not have bought that Cadillac. I am way too young to have that thing. (Note to self: sell Cadillac.)

Before I can muster up a response she decides to add insult to injury and follow up her *faux pas* with another humdinger, sure to boost her sales quota for the day. "Are you shopping for a gift?" she says.

Excuse me? I am thinking this to myself. *Do you see my hip new highlights? Did you take a peek at this killer blow-out? Do you see that I just got a freakin' spray tan? And you have the audacity to assume I am gift shopping?*

What I say aloud, very calmly and bravely is: "No, actually, I was just looking for a tank top for myself."

"Oh, of course," she says. "What size are you?"

Cue deer-caught-in-headlights look. I see her lips moving in slow motion, I know what she's asking, but I don't know how to respond. I mean, I know what size I *usually* wear, but I don't know how to honestly admit this to a teenager who probably would just as soon kill herself as see the scale tip the 100 mark. I have to think fast; I have to come up with an acceptable answer. What size *am* I? (What size am I? Well, that depends on which item of clothing we are talking about. It depends on what time of day it is. It depends on whether it is Day 5 of my new diet. It depends on whether I have endured any recent sickness that has curbed my appetite. It depends on the weather, and if I am retaining water.) I quickly rationalize: there is no correct answer to her absurd inquiry. It is truly up to interpretation.

"Ma'am, what size are you looking for?" she repeats.

I heard you, little brat. I am just thinking about my answer.

"Well, I am normally a Medium, but I think I want it to be big, so I'll take an XLarge," I say with all the confidence I can muster.

"Oh, XLarge? Okay, well, we keep those in the back. But I can get one for you."

In the *back*? Why are the human sizes kept in the back? I mean, it is obvious that anyone of normal stature is going to be asking for one. (I wonder if the store manager knows that the XLarges are housed in the back. I bet they lose a lot of sales because of that.) Anyone with a job that can afford to spend $48.00 on a freaking tank top has to be of normal proportions, I assume.

I decide to just wait for the tank top and get it to go. I need out of here. Why is the music so freaking loud in here, anyway? Who can work like this? Between the loud music and the pulverizing stench of cheap house-brand cologne, my head hurts so bad I can barely keep myself erect.

Just when I can't take it one more second, the music stops. *Wow! That's eerie.* I was just thinking the music sucked—and it stopped. (Another note to self: test these newfound mind powers again later). Oh, but my joy is short lived. The music is merely interrupted by the store intercom as Skinny Suzie makes a plea to her cohorts via her walkie-talkie.

"Candy, can you please grab me a blue tank top in an EXTRA LARGE from the stock room?"

I have been outed. Someone shoot me now. It does not take a genius to figure out that I must be the lucky winner. I do a quick scan of the potential "XL" shoppers in the place. *Nada!* I am apparently the only one who did not take The Scale Test before entering the store. By the looks of it, anyone over 105 pounds need not apply. I am drowning amongst frisky adolescents, who are probably too young to know that Madonna is a musical icon, not an author! Each of them likely has the classic "under 20" metabolism that allows them to indulge in whatever they can manage to load in a fry-daddy—and never see it settle on their hips. Well, the joke is on them, ladies and gentleman, because I, too, used to claim that genetic phenomenon. Then, I graduated from college, and look at me now, baby.

Take a long hard look at the future, sister. You will be shopping for an XLarge one day, and I am going to be there, lurking, laughing, and announcing it on the DAMN WALKIE-TALKIE!!

So now I am faced with two choices. I could bolt, make a clean break for the door while Candy is retrieving my undesirable frock from the stock room (a.k.a. "Fat Barn"). Or, I could wait for my XLarge and then try it on and announce how big it is and that I'd better just grab a Medium (no need to try the Medium on, of course). Then I could wrap the Medium up at home and give it to my ten-year-old daughter for Christmas (and she could use it to dress her American Girl dolls).

When a winded Candy (what, one flight of stairs made you tired, Miss Candy?) returns from the back with my apparent Aloha *muumuu*, I quickly advance to the dressing room. I don't make eye contact with any of the gawkers, but I could swear that I see a Japanese tourist snap a photo of "fat American woman" to show off to his cronies back home.

Once safely inside the dressing room, I stare at myself in the mirror, wasting a few minutes—which could pass for ample time to try on the tank top and get dressed again. I peep at my highlights, which don't seem to have the same luster now as they did before I stepped into this Barbie Disco-slash-clothing store. (It must be the fluorescent lighting, because I just paid $200.00 for the damn color. I know it can't be fading yet!)

Time is up! I can return to the sales floor and claim my much smaller, and much more socially acceptable "Here in Who-ville" tank top.

"Excuse me," I say. "I am *so* sorry to make you go all the way to the stock room, but this XLarge is WAY too big for me. I think I will just grab the Medium and call it good."

"Okay, then," she says with a smile, as if I am again "on her team." She leads me to the cash wrap and begins ringing up my $48.00 tank top (*why* am I buying this again?).

"You can go ahead and call Candy back, "I say firmly, "and tell her I did not need it. Tell her it was too big. Tell her she can have the XLarge back because I needed the Medium instead." Now, I'm demanding! She is not about to get away with humiliating me and then not even fix it. I am going through a lot of trouble to keep myself in denial here; the least she can do is play along. She had no qualms about shouting my size to everyone a few minutes ago, so now she needs to retract that, and let everyone know that I am NOT an XLARGE!

"Oh, that's okay," she says sweetly. "I'll just put it in the pile to take to the back after we close." And she grins. Is she mocking me? Is she doing this on purpose? Does she think this is a joke?

"No, really. I know you probably have a big enough mess at the end of the day. I can wait, really. It's no trouble. Just call her on your walkie-talkie and let her know that she can come and get the XLARGE up here, right now; it's no problem. *Really*. I am fine to wait. Go ahead." (Am I starting to sound desperate? Ever so slightly?)

Remain calm, I silently tell myself. *Don't blow your cover*. If I sound too insistent, she'll wonder why I am dead-set on her going to the stock room. She will undoubtedly assume that I am going to steal something (which would explain why someone like me would dare to show up at a store like this, knowing full well that none of the items offered here would pull up past my knees anyway). I don't want her to alert security. I wonder if department stores have those little panic buttons under the counter, like they do at the bank. That would sure be a topper to my day. I picture the headline: "Old Fat Lady Poses as Customer, Gets Arrested for Shoplifting." Nice.

"So you can just go ahead and call," I repeat.

"Uh, okay. Sure!" she says.

YES! I can see her reaching for the walkie-talkie. Victory! She is about to call Candy back to take this hideous garment out to pasture where it belongs. I certainly won't be needing it. Everyone will know the truth (well, not the "real truth," but that's no one's business anyway, right?). I am not purchasing the XLarge. Though it may look that way from a distance, Mr. Japanese Photographer, it is clearly a few sizes smaller (as am I). As soon as we clear this little matter up, I'll be on my way. Go ahead, Skinny Suzie, make my day!

"Candy, can you please come pick up the pile of go-backs for the stock room?"

Morphing into My Mother

Call it a rite of passage, but apparently, every girl at some point needs to go through it (at least that's what Oprah says). I celebrated this milestone a few months ago. I am not talking about my first experience with childbirth (I don't think I'm going to write about that in this book), and I am not talking about my wedding day (again, for another book). I am not talking about graduating from college (you already know that I did not get a degree, and also that I quit therapy so that I could finish this damn book—all so that *you* could see the humor in my truths). And I am certainly *not* discussing hitting my goal weight (this needs no commentary from the author). No. I am talking about being fitted for a bra by the "experts" at Nordstrom.

It all started on a lonely afternoon. I was piled up on the couch with a box of Wheat Thins and a diet soda. It was time for *Oprah*. This was the highly publicized episode where Oprah took her audience through the process of being properly fitted for a bra at Nordstrom. (What's the significance of going to Nordstrom, anyway? I'm sure that Macy's can hire "experts," too, right?) Oprah went on and on about how life-altering this was for her. Then she invited audience members to volunteer their testimonial to confirm her theory: namely, that many women are running around (yes, even now in *your* town) wearing the incorrect bra size. It's, like, the biggest case of misdiagnosis that you have ever seen (no pun intended)!

As I watched an hour dedicated to the proverbial boulder-holder and the risks involved with its neglect, misuse (or lack thereof), and manipulation, I couldn't help but wonder if I, too, were guilty of underestimating my womanhood. I mean, I have fully admitted that I have no business wearing those cute little demi-bras that I used to wear in high-school (sorry, Dad), which barely covered a nip and served no real purpose. There were no back biscuits to consider at age seventeen, no sausage roll, nor any other unsightly extra cargo that I had to monitor; so, a demi-bra was treating me right as far as I was concerned. As a matter of fact, if truth be told, I didn't need a damn bra: those babies would stand up on their own if I let them, but I knew even then I should at least *attempt* to look demure (when possible).

That being said, however, I was still left to ponder whether I had fully conformed to the full-figured silhouette or not. To me, that screamed *You are your mother!*

I remember being a kid and shopping with my mother when she was buying bras, and being totally grossed out by the fact that they came in a freaking box. That's right; her bras came in a box. (What kind of marketing genius makes the decision to design the clear plastic box for a woman's unmentionables, anyway?) On the outside, with its glossy picture of a "full-figured" woman, it said: "18-hour Bra."

Right then I was thinking, who wears a bra for eighteen hours? (Again, sorry Dad.) Shouldn't that holding device be coming off in, oh, at least twelve hours max? Secondly, who wants to look like that gal on the box? I'm sure she's a very nice lady, but she categorically does *not* have the market cornered on sex appeal (if you know what I mean). At the ripe old age of seventeen I was just praying to God, promising to be good, and vowing to never, *ever* purchase a bra in a box!

So it begs the original question: Was I now, at age thirty-one, finally a full-figured silhouette, or not? There was only one way to find out (as per Ms. Winfrey). So I packed up the car and my handy-dandy shopping partner, Joan, and we headed to the nearest Nordys. (Just for the record, before we get any further into this story, no matter what happens, I want you to know that I stand by what I said. There is something sick and wrong about marketing bras from a plastic box. But strangely, I seem to find those full-figured women on the boxes oddly sexy at this juncture in life).

I also feel the need to clarify one other thing before I take you, full speed, into the dressing room at Nordstrom. I did have breast augmentation surgery a full year prior to my fitting-room fiasco. To make a long story short, I once had decent size boobs, but they got a little, how shall I say . . . l-o-n-g, after I had children (can I get an *Amen* from all the moms in the crowd). So, I went to see the doctor about having a lift. He told me that I could not get a lift; he said I could get an implant to *fill up* the breast tissue, which would create the fuller look I was after. End result? Bigger . . . long boobs. What I mean is, I felt they should be a little more perky since I'd just dropped a bunch of dough on them, and technically (as per the ad in the brochure), I should be able to go bra-less without looking like a hooker. That's the *look* I was after. I would likely always wear a bra, but I did love the idea of having the option. Does that make sense? But the bulbs I had planted were like balloons, baby; there was no way I was going commando unless I was on South Beach (and even then, I'd be charging a cover)!

The point I am so graphically trying to make here is that my breasts were still a tad bit on the saggy side, considering the fact that they were fake. Interestingly, I was wearing the same bras that I wore before the surgery, which should have been my first clue that perhaps I was walking around in ill-fitting garments.

Now that you are completely caught up, let's proceed into the Nordstrom Lingerie Department with no secrets between us (unless you are keeping skeletons in your closet, that is). Here goes.

Joan and I walked into the department. I scoped out the racks of bras and panties, but nothing really caught my eye right off the bat. A nice sales girl wearing a cute pair of Capri pants and a measuring tape draped around her neck was quick to approach me (she must have taken one look at my droopy tits and known immediately that I needed attention). She asked me some basic, probing questions (obviously to see if I had a clue about this stuff) and then offered to pick me up a few choices and put them in a room for me. She asked me my size. (Note that asking a woman her bra size is much different than asking her what her pant size is. I mean, don't get me wrong, we are likely to lie in both incidences, but usually when it comes to our chest, we round *up*, and for our pant size, we round *down*. But in any event, it's not nearly as offensive to offer up the info in regards to the chest.) I told her I was a 36D.

When I was done perusing (read stalling) the rest of the department, I retired to the dressing room. My sister, Joan, entered the stall next to me (with all her perky 34C demi-bras, whatever!). The sales gal—we'll call her Helen—knocked and asked if she could come in to measure me, just to make sure she was pulling the correct size (this must be what Oprah had been raving about). I was happy to oblige.

Helen opened the door and took one look at me standing there in my bra and jeans and told me flat out that I was *not* a 36D. *Wow*, I thought to myself. I could swear I was a 36D. I mean, I'd just taken on 400 *ccs* of saline, for goodness sake—and I was no pancake before that surgery either! But, she was the "expert," so I was going to have to go with her advice. (Maybe I'd get into one of those demi-bras again, after all. I think they go up to a 34D cup, or something.) For a split second I thought about asking Helen if she was new, but I didn't want to be rude and didn't want her to feel bad, or anything. After all, she looked so cute and professional in her capri pants and measuring tape, and I'm sure Nordstrom personnel pride themselves on their extensive training program (right?), so they'd never stick someone out on the sales floor who did not know how to do basic measurements. Helen wrapped the tape around my breasts and cinched it across my front. Her brow furrowed. She let the tape go, shook it loose and measured again. Then she spoke.

"Sarah, I'm going to go get my Assistant Manager, Kim, okay? I'll be right back!"

What was that? While she skipped off to find help, I talked to Joan through the thin walls of the dressing room divider. What the heck was that about, we wondered, but we settled on the theory that Helen, in all probability, was indeed a rookie employee, and she might not be allowed to render a verdict on a customer. Perhaps she needed to log in a certain amount of measuring hours, or view a particular number of chests before she could fly a solo mission, or something like that. There are lots of jobs like that; for instance, surgeons operate (again, no pun intended) this way (hello, I watch *Grey's Anatomy*), so it would not be too far-fetched to think that Bra Fitters work on the same premise. Anyway, I wasn't going to panic about it, or anything. Instead, I waited patiently for the Assistant Manager to arrive with a more appropriate (smaller) bra.

We soon had Kim in the dressing room with us, just as cute and cheerful as Helen. So, there were three of us squeezed into tight quarters, and I was the only one nearly naked. Kim took a quick glance at me, and I swear she almost looked at me with pity (what is *that* about). She maneuvered the measuring tape around me. (If you've never tried this, next time you're on an airplane, take two strangers into the bathroom with you and measure each other's boobs. You'll know what I mean by small spaces.)

As if on cue, Kim's brow furrowed (where do they learn that—a training video, or something?) and let go of the tape. "Ya, you're not a 36D. I'm sorry, Sarah, but I'm going to need to get the manager for this. I'll be right back."

WHAT?!?

At this point I could hear Joan roaring with laughter from the next stall. She was not even trying to hold it in. I was pretty sure that if I took the time to bend over and look, I'd see her on the floor, doubled over. Trouble was, I didn't know what was so funny—yet.

Then, I heard a knock on the door; it was the manager, Grace. "Sarah, can I come in?"

"Ye-e-e-s." Grace was slightly larger (thank God, someone who'd understand me), also cute and complete with measuring tape.

"Sorry about all this measuring," she said smoothly. "We just want to make sure we get it right. I've been doing this a long time, and whenever the girls get a difficult case, they always call me."

Case? So, now I'm a case? What constituted a case, I wondered. I didn't even want to ask, so I just assumed the correct position. I knew the drill: arms up!

"Okay," she said, "you're a 34 . . . (I was liking where her head was at) QUAD."

"I'm sorry, what did you say?"

"You're a QUAD, Sarah. A 34G. In Bra-Speak, that's a 34DDDD."

"Huh?"

"Yes Ma'am, a 34G. I'll have the girls pull some bras for you to try." And with that, she must have done some major hand signals, or something, because Helen and Kim scurried out of the dressing room on a mission without a moment to spare. It was as if the manager had hit some kind of red panic button on my fitting room door, or run a "code blue" out to the sales floor so that the entire staff could drop what they were doing to assist the girl with the enormous tits in getting a properly fitting undergarment (something in a box, perhaps). Silence filled the room that, moments before, had been littered with sales force and management (and probably people writing the training manual for "expert fitters," hunkered down in some nearby corner, eavesdropping and taking notes).

Silence, that is, except for the snorts and belly laughs erupting from the adjacent dressing room. Joan was not even attempting to control her hysterics.

"Did she say *Quad*? Sarah, you have got to be shitting me!"

Luckily for me, I didn't have to have a conversation with Joan at this time, because the Three Musketeers arrived with my Rack-Slings, and I was going to be trying them on. These gals were "experts," so I was sure the bras would at least be cute (wrong!). I quickly came to the realization that I had exactly *one* choice of bra when it came to the quad variety. It seems that manufacturers reckon if you have boobs that big, then you ought to put on a sports bra and a T-shirt and call it good—because *pretty* left you a long time ago, baby!

So, there I was trying on my *one* choice of bra. (Although I did get to choose from about four colors. Does that count?) As I was squirming into it, Kim decided that she'd better show me the proper way to put on a bra. (Why Kim? Maybe the three of them played rock-paper-scissors and she lost, maybe she drew the short straw, I don't know; but Kim got the job of delivering the news to the already semi-suicidal customer that, not only was she morphing into her mother—doomed to a life of buying ugly, full-figured box bras—but now she needed help learning how to maneuver her lady melons into the freaking quad-sacks, too.) As politely as she could, Kim simultaneously demonstrated and explained that I needed to first bend over and shake my breasts down into the cup, fasten the closure in the back, stand up, adjust the straps to a comfortable resistance, then make sure the back of the bra strap was resting parallel to the floor and not riding up on my back. (Well look at that, one gal's humiliation is another gal's time saver. Now you don't have to archive a whole episode of *Oprah* to get the gist of properly fitting your bra, do you?)

It was my turn to try this whole process. I bent my knees and tried to shake my boobs into the damn bra. Right away I started having flashbacks of my mother (this is no shit, you guys). Every time I saw my mother get dressed she used to shake her boobs into her (boxed) bra. Then she'd take her left hand and shove in the remainder of the right boob, which was muffin topping out of the (boxed) bra, along with the right hand; then she'd do the same to the other side. It was like clockwork. I remember it vividly because I used to sit on the bed and watch in amazement. Her boobs were huge (they were probably, like, DDs for God sakes)! Then she would take her hands and run them all the way inside her nude-colored pantyhose (which came nestled inside an egg-shaped plastic container from the grocery store), wedge her feet in the toes, snake that hose all the way up one leg, then repeat it all on the other side.

Isn't it strange the things we remember from childhoods (stranger yet, the things that scar us for life)? To this day, I have yet to wear nude-colored pantyhose. But in my mom's defense, I think this has more to do with the style and less to do with her. That whole purchasing undergarments from the grocery store thing, however—that's an issue I'll take to the grave (not going to happen).

So it goes without saying that when cute little Kim asked me to bend over and shake my *ta-tas* into the bra, I instantly felt like I'd morphed into my mother. Kim might as well ring me up for a lifetime supply of boxed bras; she might as well call me Mrs. Cleland because I had become my mother.

I could deal with the quad issue. I mean, I knew that as soon as Joan stopped laughing long enough to catch her breath she'd let me cry on her shoulder. Or, I could always call my other sister, Jeni (who shares my mother's genes and who would undoubtedly bust a gut as well, but she'd be able to keep me out of therapy, at least), and then I could work through my issues with her, too.

For what it's worth, I still believe in Oprah. She does great work and she has some interesting things to share. I still believe in Nordstrom (that goes without saying). I still see the benefit of going to the lingerie department and getting fitted by the "expert" and making sure that I'm wearing the bra that will best support my lady lumps so that I won't be inadvertently prone to any premature sagging. However, I am defiantly an advocate for boycotting the sale of any undergarment in the same facility that sells turkey, peanut butter, and light bulbs (and on a side note, *any* undergarment that comes in a plastic egg or a plastic box, no matter where it's sold).

Lastly, I think I'd like to give a shout out to the model on the 18-Hour Bra box. Girl, I can see now that it wasn't so much that you *could* wear that bra for eighteen hours, it was more that you *had* to wear that bra for eighteen hours—to avoid all kinds of back pain, joint tension, and muscle spasms. So I get it now! And I want to say thank you; you are beautiful. I also want you to consider that it might be time for you to, well . . . think *outside* the box for a change!

3

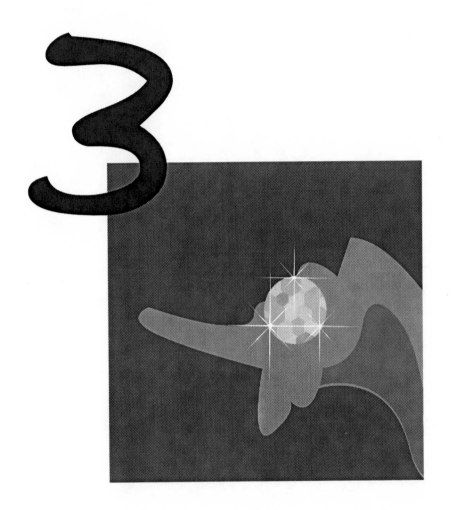

T.G.I.F

I love Fridays. I love Fridays for lot of reasons. I like the fact that they signal the start of the weekend, which usually means I don't have to wear make-up for a few days (which I guess also suggest that I don't have a life—but we can dissect that in a later chapter). Fridays also mean that I get to sleep in for two days in a row; plus, the new movies come out in the local theater. But perhaps the best thing about Fridays is that these are the days I indulge in my secret little obsession (I know what you're thinking, and it is not a hot fudge sundae). So what is this passion? The newest editions of my favorite news magazines hit the stands!

Now, let me clarify for any scholars who might be reading this book that my idea of news and your idea of news might differ. I mean the "news": you know, *In Touch, US Weekly, People Magazine,* the real news mags. You would think it was my birthday by the way I rush out to the store to pick up my copy of the latest gossip. It's addicting.

I've often wondered why I care so much about people's lives, people I have never even met. I conclude that it goes back to my inner longing to be a soap opera star (if there are any casting agents for *Days of Our Lives* reading this, call me). For as long as I can remember, I have wanted to move to Los Angeles and be a soap star. I've always been told that I am dramatic (perfect), I love attention, and I would *so* be into kissing hot guys and getting paid for it!

Anyway, I think it is safe to assume at this juncture that being a soap star is not in the cards for this drama queen. So, what's the next best thing? Reading about other people in Hollywood's ridiculous rivalries, catfights, drug abuse cases, and lawsuits!

One thing I have noticed, however, is that over time I have assumed the role of counselor for some of these people. It's like I think I really know them, or something. I find myself calling up my friends (also avid readers; we tend to flock together) and cueing them in on the fact that Nick and Jess broke up, and how "I called it" way back in June. Then I proceed to explain all the reasons why it was inevitable, who they should date next, and what *really* happened to end the relationship (as if I have the inside scoop).

My husband shakes his head at me every Friday when he catches me reading up on the weekly news. He wonders why anyone would spend so much of her time investing in someone else's drama (is he serious?). And this is coming from someone who reads the local newspaper (snooze) and calls reviewing a road atlas entertainment (lame).

A few weeks ago, as I was on my way home from getting my weekly fix, I had to literally pull the car over to read the cover story. I could not wait. It was a story about a celeb (who shall remain nameless), and the interviewer was complimenting her on her recent weight loss. Now, since I, too, know what it's like to struggle with weight, I figured I better find out which magic potion Little Miss Hollywood got her hands on—and how much it was going to cost me.

I flipped through the pages to find the article, and there she was in a big glossy with "before" and "after" captions in bold print. Let me just say that "before" was, like, three months prior to the photo-op, so we were not talking a long interim here. And there it was: her quote. The juicy tidbit of information that could single-handedly transform my life, ushering me into a svelte new realm. She'd done it in just three months. I could do it, too. She had lost *seventy* pounds, and I couldn't wait to read the secret.

"I just cut out French fries and switched to diet soda," she explained.

Uh, hello! Was anyone else thinking what I was thinking? Like, did she replace the fries with cocaine? I am sorry, but no one loses seventy freaking pounds in three freaking months by "cutting out the fries"—unless she's been setting up camp in Burger King (which I knew *for a fact* was not true because she was out at the Ivy every night with some married music producer.) No ones eats that many fries in the first place. Secondly, she admitted switching to diet soda. Okay, what was she drinking before, drawn butter?

Answers like these are so depressing, and they make me so mad. Why couldn't she just call a spade a spade, and admit she was on meth? Everyone knows it anyway, Little Miss Hot Pants; you are starving yourself because you have a video shoot (or something random like that) and you want all of mankind (including my husband) lining up to sleep with you. That's what it is! You don't want the paparazzi blowing up your ass and putting your image on the cover of some slick magazine underneath the caption "Even the Hollywood Elite Have Cellulite" (which would probably make me respect you again, anyway). So instead, you insult my intelligence and come up with some cockamamie story that losing weight has something to do with cutting back on America's proverbial junk food. Puh-leeze! You probably have a publicist who comes up with this B.S. because he gets some kind of bonus based on your waistline (and everyone knows that a junkie has no marketability), so you voluntarily endure a liquid diet to attain a date with a boy-bander—all to score the cover of *Star* so that people like me can have something to bitch about. Thanks for taking one for the team.

Well, like I said, all this happened a few weeks ago. I pulled back into traffic, deciding that I could wait until I got home to read the rest of that issue. I did, however, decide to skip the drive-thru that day (just in case there was any truth to her theory), opting to starve myself—for a few hours, at least. I may have wondered what would happen to me if I cut out cake for three months. I can tell you today what would happen if I *ate* cake for three months (hypothetically, of course): I'd gain eleven pounds in the first three weeks, and then I'd go shopping. Not good shopping, mind you, but the kind of shopping you must do after you bust the zipper out of your favorite (fat) jeans. I would then spend the remaining nine months of the year trying to lose the eleven pounds of back-biscuits that took a mere three weeks to pack on (again, hypothetically).

That's why I find it really hard to believe that any human being could lose seventy pounds in three months without the use of illegal narcotics. There, I said it (you were thinking it, too).

So if week after week I am bombarded with images of airbrushed stick-women in hooker boots, lying about the truth in their lives, why do I rush out to buy these rags? It is like a soap opera. Each week I pick up the new edition (kind of pathetic, I know) to see what has transpired since the last installment. I like to see what they're wearing (especially who ends up on the worst-dressed list). I like to see the new hairstyles, and who was caught cheating on whom. It is an opportunity to be involved in something totally removed from normal suburban life, yet I don't have to own it. Now that I say that out loud, I can really see how feeble it sounds. But for $2.99, I can sit on the couch (with some bon bons) and escape into another world. I can forget about my troubles (you think you have problems?—look at TomKat) for an hour or two and be part of the elite crowd.

Then, when I have had my fill, I close the magazine. I can look lovingly at my children (because there is no nanny to take them) as they practice their bible verses and pet the cat (because normal people have cats, not "purse dogs"), and the cat purrs and purrs contentedly on my lap. I can gaze out the window at the beautiful, serene view of the mountains (because I live in the toolies) and wait for my loving (non-cheating) husband to come home from work (unlike KFed, he has a J.O.B.), and maybe—just maybe—I can be content, just being me.

(Meanwhile, Ben and Jen *aren't* really on the rocks; Vince has *not* proposed to the other Jen, but I know (for a fact) that he will soon; and "Brangelina" is all a hoax to boost movie sales. (She is a lesbian, and Brad really pines for me.)

My First Time

I remember it as if it were only a meal ago. My first time. It was all that I thought it would be.

I'd never been the type to really plan it out, detail for detail. I mean, truth be told, I never gave it much thought at all. It was one of those things that I knew was inevitable (after all I was a living, breathing woman who had needs), but I was in no hurry to close the deal with "just anyone." It had to be the right person at the right time. All of the factors that were important to me had to be aligned. I'm not going to lie, looks are important. I know—within one glance—whether or not I'm attracted (for more than just a one-time use, that is). Also, I don't care what they say, *size does matter*. When I'm on the prowl, I expect to find the perfect size, almost as if it were made just for me.

On this particular day the planets were all aligned and God was on my side. It was as if He had whispered to me, "You've been so obedient and patient; it's time for the payoff." It was an icy November night. I remember that the thermometer in my car read twenty-one degrees. I'd just decorated my Christmas tree, and I was basking in the stillness and wonder of freshly fallen snow. I guess you could say it was written in the stars. It was my night. I admit I was a little nervous at first, but I told myself to ease into it and let passion be my guide. I, at the ripe age of thirty-one, finally felt like a woman.

I am talking, of course, about the first time I purchased a handbag on eBay (get your mind out of the gutter, pervert!). For those of you who've experienced the novelty, you're picking up what I'm puttin' down right now. If you've never done it, then I encourage you to put this book down and log on. Go. I'll wait. (Why are you still reading? Go!)

Okay, now I feel like we're on the same playing field. I can't go on describing this milestone to someone who has no idea what I'm talking about. It's like trying to describe sex to a virgin: It does not compute (in fact, it might even gross you out).

So, back to my story.

I eased into my first eBay experience by typing in some broad searches, like "handbags" and "women's shoes." After I got comfortable, I scaled things down to a more refined criterion, such as *"Prada shoes"* and *"Chloe handbags"*. I was awe-struck by all the choices. They were displayed in the order of time remaining in the auction, so some of the items were closing within minutes. (I found this too stressful and had to start with items that at least had an hour remaining. I can't make a qualified decision in three minutes.)

I found several bags I liked. So I did what you would call "watch" them. That means that when you click on them, they come up on your personal screen so you can keep an eye on them, see if you want to bid, increase your bid, etc. Lo and behold, I guess I wasn't as picky as I thought because within twelve minutes, I was "watching" thirty-six handbags! This was like shooting fish in a barrel. I was shopping in my PJ's, with my husband's credit card (sorry Honey, I'll make it up to you when this damn book goes Bestseller) at one o'clock in the morning. Does life get any better? It wasn't long before I'd grasped the fact that this was serious business and I'd better get my game face on (brew some coffee, this is gonna be a long night). These players were on a mission. Bids were coming in from all over the world. Items were falling off, new items were coming on, and I was right in the middle of this glorious mayhem of the Global Mall (sweet Jesus, I think I just had an orgasm).

It started out as a friendly flirtation. I was looking at several handbags. You know, playing the field. I had money to spend, but I wasn't going to throw it at the first item that piqued my interest. I was playing my hand close to the vest. Cautious. Alert. Strategic. I had my eye on the bag that I thought would be the "one" (FYI: if by chance it didn't work out with us, I did have a back up plan). It was an "authentic" black leather *Chloe* handbag to die for. I had seen Mary Kate Olsen carrying one on the pages of *US Magazine* (you know how I feel about *US Magazine*) a few months back. It was even labeled as "the must-have bag of the season" (wonder which season, exactly), and that, as you know, is my language. There were seven hours and forty-six minutes left in the auction for this bag. Now according to my calculations, that would extend the bidding well into the night, and it would expire sometime around 7:00 o'clock in the morning, my time. The bidding started at $200.00. (I know, a little pricey for my first purchase but remember, *husband's* credit card—and it was an $1800.00 handbag, so technically I'd just *saved* my husband $1600.00. Yay me!)

After I placed my bid, I had to go into wait-and-see mode. This is where, to use Cyber-speak, you just "refresh" every three minutes or so to see if you're still the winning bidder. If someone outbids you, then you need to bid again. This dance continues until the time expires and the best woman wins.

Since I had some time to kill, I figured I should spend it perusing the other items available on eBay (wouldn't want to log off and spend time with the family or clean something). So I checked out ski pants (for my son), Christmas ornaments (again, for the family to enjoy), GPS systems (on my husband's Christmas list), and then, somehow, I ended up back at shoes (oops! I did it again). There were some "hot" *Prada* pumps that were screaming my name. You would've bid on them, too. The shoes had nine hours left in the auction, so I placed my bid and then continued to "look" around.

I didn't realize how much time had gone by, but apparently my husband, Brian, did. He came into my office a few times and asked me if I was (ever) coming to bed. Of course, when he entered the room I quickly minimized the screen so that he didn't know I was shopping (I'm not stupid). Although, I'm not sure what he thought I was doing because, every time he came in, I was just starring at my desktop icons in amazement (I can never pull up a new website in a timely manner when I'm under pressure). Lucky for me, he never pointed that fact out and just let me continue the madness. By this time, it was 1:46 a.m., there were still a few hours left in the handbag auction, and so far, I was still the winning bid.

Don't get me wrong, I did take a break for a piece of cold pizza, to go to the bathroom, to let the cat in from the cold, and even to catch the last few minutes of my soap opera (which plays again at night on *SoapNet*). But it's fair to say that I did spend the majority of seven or eight hours glued to my 15-inch monitor. So long in fact, that the back of my neck felt like I had a brick resting on it. I felt massive muscle strain and tension (likely from anxiety), and I made a note to myself to schedule a much-needed massage for the following day. On-line shopping is a real shit kicker on the ole body.

For those of you who can't connect the dots, let me spell this out for you. In a matter of hours, I had placed about seventeen bids on multiple handbags, shoes (random stuff that I knew I'd never use, but it was such a good deal that I could not pass it up), and home décor. It's all fun and games until you realize that you might actually *win* all these items; meaning that you might have to *pay* for all these items (or your husband, whichever the case may be). If I actually won these items, it would not be such a good thing. I had about $2700.00 on the table, and Daddy was not coming to my rescue on this one.

I did what any other self-respecting thirty-one-year-old woman would do at this juncture: I frantically searched the website for the Rules and Regulations (loop hole) to find the policy about deleting a placed bid (it was either that, or move to Mexico). Unfortunately, however, after several minutes and countless clicks of the mouse, it was evident that there was no way to take back my bid. I just had to wait it out. This was not good. (I wondered if you could get a good divorce attorney on eBay. Well, I certainly had the time to find out.)

It was amazing to me how quickly I'd been sucked in. Sure, at first glance it all seems harmless. Here is this huge network of buyers and sellers from all over the world bringing goods and services (and I do mean "goods") to your fingertips (literally). For a gal who loves to shop, it's like dropping a kid off at the candy store with a Platinum American Express card (Mommy's AMEX, of course) and letting the kid camp out there for the night. The kid is not thinking about how quickly his teeth will rot, or how bad his stomach will ache in the morning. He's all about the instant gratification of being able to indulge in harmless doses of Hubba Bubba and Red Ropes. Add in the fact that I had been cooped up in my house for three days due to an untimely snowstorm, AND the fact that it was the holiday season and everything around me was a subliminal invitation to shop (To: *Me*; From: *Me*), and I didn't have a snowball's chance in hell of abstaining! (I am but a puppet, folks, in eBay's quest to rule the world.)

Sure, I'd gone my whole life without it; I'd never even really considered the option, much less the ramifications of shopping on eBay. I guess I was under the impression that eBay was like an international garage sale, a venue where people sold their junk because their homes were going into foreclosure, or something. At best, you were lucky to pick up some random antique that your Grandmother collected when you were a kid. You felt good about throwing a few bucks out to get it (make Grandma proud), all for the sentimental value (plus the idea that you were helping to keep the roof over someone's head was a bonus, too). I could never have anticipated the life-changing effect it would have on me. Now, I would never shop the same way again. (Who, in their right mind, would pay full price?).

I could just see myself in the future. I would morph into "Thrifty Sarah." Anytime anyone needed something I would be the gal saying, "Wait, I can get that soooo much cheaper on eBay!" Soon to follow would be a new persona: "Recycle Sarah"; she would be the version of me that went through her own closet to find all the stuff that might bring in some major dough at the auction (hey, one man's junk is another man's treasure). Then perhaps I would quietly slide into "Pathetic Sarah," the me that would go through my friends' closets, asking questions like, "Do you still fit in that?" or "I'll take those Goodwill bags for you!" Let us not forget the expansion to "Entrepreneur Sarah." This is the me that will hatch the grand idea to start my own eBay Store. I will live as a hermit with carpal tunnel and a neck brace, spending my days rummaging garage sales for "treasure" and my nights monitoring the other social defects who stay up late to post bids. ("This is your life. *This is your life on eBay.*") Glorious!

So here's the moral of the story, boys and girls. Never underestimate the power of a virtual mall that is open 24/7 and resides in your own home. If you haven't tried it already, don't do it. Don't even get started. But if you must (I get it, everyone wants their own story about their first time), you should at least benefit from a few things that I've learned.

First, the really experienced people on eBay love to toy with the newbies. Sure, they let you think you're going to win the bid. They let you do your silly celebratory dance, call your friends, and send out the link to the "new shoes you just won." But in an instant, when it's quiet and there are only a few seconds left to bid (and you're already searching the auction for the new skirt you need to go with your new shoes), out of the shadows they pounce. They outbid you by three cents, and you don't have any time to react. Just like that, you lose, sister. Easy come, easy go. You're out! Pissed off, you immediately go to work to find "the next best thing" (after all, you still have money to spend). The cycle continues. It can suck you in, like a moth to a flame, girlfriend.

Secondly, EVERYTHING can be sold on eBay. I even heard about a gal who bought a single piece of Key Lime Pie on eBay. She had it shipped all the way from Florida to Washington. The pie cost her about eight dollars, and then she paid, like, $19.99 for overnight shipping (everyone likes to enjoy fresh pie now and then)! If you think it's junk, it isn't. If you think no one will want it, you're wrong. If Britney Spears can bottle up her sweat and pull in $1200.00 for it, then I vote that I should take a swing with my "previously loved" Dooney and Burke bag, okay?

Oh, and by the way, for those of you who will not heed my warning about this cyber-superstore, the answer is "yes." Yes, you can get a divorce attorney on eBay. I can't give you any names, however, because, fortunately for me, I got out before it was too late!

The Biggest Fish
I Ever Saw

I grew up without one. And I'm normal (well, for the most part). I never had to sit on a stranger's couch and confess some deep-rooted struggle that swirled around the fact that I never owned a dog as a child. I still managed to find other ways to demonstrate responsibility in my life (like, oh I don't know, finding a job). I also, believe it or not, figured out other ways to manifest loving relationships—with real live *Homo sapiens*, and even some imaginary ones, as the case may be. Why is it that animal lovers think that you are "missing out" on something if you don't have pets? Maybe this assumption parallels the same kind of sickness one finds in parents. If you have kids, then you just can't imagine what life would be like without them, and you feel like your friends without kids are really missing out on "true" happiness. (Let me translate that for you, by the way: if your kids are over the age of two, what that really means is that we parents are *jealous*. We long for the days when we did not have kids and we could go to movies that were not animated, and we could shop without a stroller, and we could enjoy a three-course meal at a restaurant, where the menus did not come with crayons and paper tablecloths. Don't be fooled by our sad eyes and our school fundraiser catalogs.)

On the other end of the spectrum, the people who don't have kids think life is complete just the way it is. The very thought of giving up their freedom is enough to send them running to the bottle (Jack Daniels, that is). They are accustomed to getting their own needs met and are not keen on the idea of catering to someone else 24/7, especially someone who does not even have the wherewithal to send you a "thank you" latté after a sleepless night (rude), or a battle with baby blues (gasp), or something of that nature.

I've learned that it is much the same with pets. Being a person who was raised without one, and who also managed to escape unscathed, I have always felt that if I got hit by a bus tomorrow, I would be okay with the fact that I never knew the much-hyped warm-fuzzy bond with a consenting canine. That is, until I needed to get a fish. Let the record show that, on a fateful day in January, when I finally broke down and agreed to get my son a few fish (for the tank that he had gotten for Christmas from his uncle), all our lives changed.

As you may have guessed, on Christmas day, when a five-year-old boy opens a big box housing a five-gallon fish tank, *excited* does not even begin to describe the emotion this boy feels. He is *elated*. So when you do the math and realize it is the end of January before we are on the way to the pet store to get the freaking fish, you should note that this is how much I *do not* want fish in my house. I mean, don't get me wrong, it is nothing personal toward the little guys; I just know that this is more work for Mom (thanks, Uncle Russ).

Getting a kid a fish tank is right up there with getting him a drum set (all parents know what I'm talking about). It will be work for me because I am the one who is going to have to clean the tank, feed the fish, make sure that all is well in the underwater ecosystem, and ultimately flush the ones who don't make the cut (hey, survival of the fittest, baby). Remember, I don't even really like animals, so now every time one of those little slime-ohs goes belly-up, I'm going to have to pretend to give a shit and conduct some kind of fish funeral at the toilet, then say a prayer as we flush the big Kohler and send Flipper off to fishy heaven (I can do it once; but I can see it getting *really* old, *really* fast). But somewhere in the Mom Handbook it clearly states that if your son gets a fish tank as a gift, then you *must* allow (trust me, I looked for the loop hole; rock solid) the fish to reside in the home. So (seven weeks later), off to the pet store we went.

As we walked into the pet store that night, the smell instantly reminded me of all the reasons I never had pets. It was no ordinary pet store. Don't visualize Pet Smart, or anything. No sir, it was more like a feed store housed in a barn that also happened to supply fish in the back (why the hell not). It stunk to high heaven in there. If that weren't enough to make me want to run for cover, the piercing sounds of birds chirping, dogs barking, hens clucking, and cats bellowing sure did. Good God, it was like the Farmer-in-the-Dell on steroids. The kids thought it was great (they would), and I was being careful not to rub my $200.00 jacket up against any furry critter that might leave some undesirable pheromone markings on my sleeve. We were on a mission: get the fish and get out.

I had planned to breeze by the puppy room, but then I happened to see their cages stacked on top of each other. Each one held two or three puppies, yelping and jumping about, banging against the bars. They were all vying for the attention of the few passersby, hoping to catch the eye of someone (a sucker) to take them home. I felt the familiar tug at my leg, and my son asked if he could take a closer look at the doggies. As a family, we stopped to observe the dogs—just for a minute (mistake *número uno*).

From the back of the pile in one of the cages, a little brown nose made its way toward the front. At the top of that nose glowed the sweetest pair of milk chocolate-brown eyes that ever belonged to a miniature dachshund, and he stared right into my soul. Although I didn't say a thing, he knew he was going to come home with us. Cute? He was perfect. I am not sure why I felt a connection to this animal: all I knew was that he needed to be a part of our family. My kids must've sniffed out my emotion because they were all over it. They took one look at me and capitalized on my moment of weakness. (They know how to strike while the iron is hot, if you know what I mean.) Within moments, they had me convinced that my husband would love the dog, too, that they would take care of it, that they would do all their chores without being told, and that I would forever be their favorite mother (hey, wait a minute . . .). Somewhere in all the frenzy, I agreed to talk to my husband about getting the dog. For the first time in my life I was considering crossing over to the other side: to pet owner.

Needless to say, once we got home my children (God bless 'em) staged Oscar-worthy performances for my husband—who is not a fan of little dogs, in the least. Amazingly, he also agreed to allow

"Duke" to join our household. So the next morning at nine o'clock sharp I went back to the pet store to claim my baby, Duke, and bring him home for good.

This is where it really gets interesting. I mentioned that I was never a pet owner. So, to say that I don't know much about dogs is an understatement. To say that I don't run in pet breeder circles is a major understatement. When I walked in to get that little pup, I had *no idea* what I was getting myself into.

I sauntered up to the front counter (simultaneously having a full-on conversation on my cell phone, of course) and told the nice lady that I would like to take the "little dachshund" home. She looked at me, puzzled (obviously never having seen me in the store before), and she asked, "Have you *held* the doxie yet?"

"The what?" I asked, confused.

"The dog. Have you held that dog yet?"

"Oh, ya. I was here last night and held her. She's pretty cute. My kids want her, so I think we'll get her," I clarified. (I was a little annoyed I might add. Couldn't she see I was *on the phone?*)

"Okay. Well, *she* is a *he*, first of all. And you say you have kids? How old?" she asked.

"Oh, five and ten," I said, as I told my friend Jessica I'd call her back in a "sec," after I took care of this whole puppy issue.

"Okay then. I will have someone go get the dog. You can start filling out the paperwork."

Paperwork? Wonder why I need to fill our paperwork, I thought to myself. *I mean, I'm getting a dog, not adopting a child, right?* But I was sure that they'd need a record of where the dog lived, in case it got lost (that would make sense), and to know where to send any coupons for doggy food, and such (maybe there was even a little newsletter, or something).

"Have you ever owned a dachshund?"

"No. Never even had a dog! Can you believe it? This is a total whim!" I confessed.

Her eyes grew dim. She cocked her head to one side as if about to speak, then she stopped herself. She put down her pen and stepped out from behind the counter, heading straight toward me.

"You have never had a dog? This is a whim?" she repeated, accusingly. Her eyes darted back and forth, as if hoping for a glimpse of some damn sign that spelled out her rights as an adoption agency. There had to be some legal loophole to save her (or the puppy), some way to stop this transaction. I could see it on her face; she was genuinely worried about the well-being of this pup (as if she were sending him off to reside with Cruella Deville, or something).

Why, all of a sudden, did *I* feel bad? I mean, if *I* didn't adopt this puppy, wasn't something really bad going to happen to him? Why was she making me feel like a total loser for wanting to give this puppy a nice life? Was she expecting me to take Puppy Parenting classes first? Should I be going to Puppy Counseling Sessions to make sure I *really* wanted a puppy before I committed to bringing one home? It was a freakin' dog, for God sakes. What was the big deal? He was a three-pound ball of fun, a little bundle of shit and giggles that I was promising to love and feed. Wasn't that enough for me to get him in the car, for crying out loud? (Scouts honor, lady. Now wrap him up and let's get on with it; I have a nail appointment, damn it)!

Still, I tried to reassure her. "Well, I mean, I have never really wanted a dog until now. But I want this dog. So I guess it's meant to be (right?)." I justified myself in an attempt to retract my previous (an obviously offensive) statement of fact.

Maybe it was not the best time to bring this up, but I thought she should know that I didn't know anything about dogs, either (maybe she guessed) and that I was going to need a little help in this area. Perhaps she would admire my honesty, and I could win back some points with my integrity. Maybe she'd find my näiveté somewhat endearing (wrong).

In retrospect, I could've spent a tad more time formulating my thoughts before I spoke, because in all of my brilliance the best I came up with, under all this pressure (who knew this would be a freaking interview?), was "Oh, um, I'm going to need some . . . er, *things* to make . . . *it*, like, you know . . . *work*." That's right: *things* (meaning food, toys, and the like), *it* (meaning their precious puppy), and *work* (meaning survive at least week one with me: Cruella).

She did not look amused. She didn't seem to interpret my lingo, if you know what I mean. Not only did I fail to gain any ground with this broad, now she was looking at me as if she were contemplating making a call to her home girls at the Animal Shelter, or something. Perhaps she would red-flag my address as soon as I left the premises (I mean, admittedly, it's not exactly Dr. Doolittle around my house, but I reckon even *I* can figure out how to keep a three-pound canine kicking, for at least a few good years).

This must have been the straw that broke the camel's back, because now the sales lady was about to school me in pet owner etiquette. Apparently you didn't joke about these things, and you also did not buy a puppy on a whim. Among the other lessons I would learn that day: you don't let the puppy outside to go potty unattended, because there must be a demand for them on the black market, or something, and everyone knew this but me. How did

I find this out, you ask? That conversation went something like this:

> ME: "So, like, when it needs to pee, can it use the cat box, or will it go outside?"
>
> PET STORE NAZI: "Well, it won't use a cat box because it's a dog. And do you have a fenced yard?"
>
> ME: "No, but my front yard is good sized, and the whole front lot is water, so the little fella won't get too far that way, even if he wants to!" (This is followed by nervous laughter—that is not reciprocated, mind you.)
>
> PET STORE NAZI: "You don't want to let him out alone without a fence. Someone will steal him."
>
> ME: "Ha! Good one. (No one laughs). Are you serious? Who would want to steal a dog? Aren't people, like, taking their dogs to the dump, and stuff, leaving them on the side of the road (digging a deeper whole for myself). Why would anyone actually steal a dog? If someone wants to go through all that, then they can have him!" (Someone, stick a fork in me; I'm done.)
>
> PET STORE NAZI: "People will steal him, re-chip him, and sell him. So just keep him safe, okay?"

Another lesson I learned that day was that dogs are not cheap. I am not sure if I even thought about the costs involved with adding a new little member to the family, but I surely didn't consider that I would need a calculator and a law degree to close this transaction. Not only did I need all the necessities to make him *work*, but the damn pup cost a cool grand (he better be able to potty train himself for that kind of cash).

But here is the kicker. Toward the end of this whole fiasco (I had been in this barn for almost an hour, mistakenly assuming I'd be in and out; I think I even left my car running in the parking lot), the sales lady handed me the "papers" for my review. These papers consisted of the history of the dog. I was expecting the pedigree to be pretty brief, considering the dog was only eight weeks old (wrong). She laid a booklet on the counter with some photos of a few other dogs on it (cute) and some words (I still don't know what they said because I did not even read them), and then I opened it up. I about shit myself. It was the dog's family tree. Typed. Complete: names, dates, birth dates. The Whole Kit and Caboodle. It went back ten (10) generations!

I don't know about you, but I don't even know my own family tree like that. If you look in my kids' baby books, you will see maternal grandparents, paternal grandparents, maybe a great-grandparent if you are lucky, an odd auntie and uncle, here and there . . . but that's about it. (And that's only for the first kid. Everyone knows that the book for the second kid just says "see sister's book for info on family.") There was even a full color picture of the puppy's parents in these "papers"—Mommy looking sweet with a daisy in her ear (what is this, a puppy Glamour Shot?), and Daddy sporting a bandana around his neck, looking very dapper and, well, studly I guess (I do see the resemblance).

I can't figure out why, on God's green earth, I would need this information. Why do I need to know when my dog's Great, Great, Great, Great Uncle Fritz Von Fralu was born? Do I really care about his Great Grand Dam, Paulina Sue Pockets? Oh, and lets all observe a moment of silence for his Great Grand Sire, Mr. Crunchier, who died on November 13, 1993. Give me a break! Maybe all the hullabaloo helps the sellers of purebred dogs sleep at night and feel *legit*, knowing they are charging people like me (who are clueless to this Canine Cult) a thousand dollars for a dog that is going to walk around my house and leave "deposits" on my new carpet for the next few years (if he is lucky)!

Maybe I should have stuck with the original plan: a fish. When you get a fish, at least you get what you pay for. It costs about four bucks, and you get about four bucks' worth of entertainment. And then they die. They swim in circles in a tank, and you promise to feed them every day. They don't disappoint you if you don't disappoint them. There's a mutual respect, of sorts. Sure, they don't come up and lick your face, and you can't blame your stinky farts on them when you have company, but there is no drama with fish (and no early morning trips outside in the cold to go poop).

All cynicism aside, it has been five days now since "the sale," and I'm happy to report that all is well. Duke, the doxie, is still alive and kicking. He loves us and we love him. Even though we joke that I'm not a dog person, I think maybe it just took the right dog to bring it out in me. We did get fish, too, and they are still swimming. Every day I look to make sure we don't have any floaters; so far, so good. I may never really understand the whole dog-breeding phenomenon, and Duke may never know any brothers or sisters (or Great Grand Sires), but he'll always know the love of his very own Cruella DeVille. So I guess the moral of this story is: be careful what you fish for, 'cause you just might get it!

Dog For Sale

We have had Duke for about six weeks now and I am *so* over it. Needless to say, this whole pet owner shindig is overrated (and underpaid). It is a full-time job and, I might say, a thankless one. When I was buying our little puppy, nowhere in the fine print on his *papers* did it talk about all the upkeep for this little five-pounder (in the real world, they call that "bait and switch," my friends).

At first he was so cute that I could overlook the fact that all he did was eat and shit on the carpet. Even his little turds were cute. They were so small and well placed (right out in the open) that I almost had to smile. It was as if he wanted to get caught; he truly didn't know any better. But the honeymoon was short lived because before the ink was dry on the check for our little purchase, Duke was ruling the roost at our house. I was on my damn knees every hour on the hour, scrubbing some kind of stinky stain from my brand new carpet or sopping up a puddle of doggy potty from my freshly mopped kitchen.

The real question was this: where were all my eager, pint-sized volunteers who, only days before, were begging me to buy the little canine in the first place? Where were those little kids who were vowing to love him, take care of him, play with him, feed him, and clean up *every* mess he made in the house? They looked at me blankly when I asked them to walk the dog, as if they could not believe that I would try to pass off *my* duties by asking them to *walk my dog*! HELLO! All their excitement for the dog had been swapped for the Nintendo and the iPod, quicker than you can say "MOM IS A SUCKER."

So, my new routine as a pet owner meant that I had to set my alarm for 3:00 a.m. every morning so that I could let Duke out to go to the bathroom. Every time I'd open the door to his "room," I would send up a silent prayer that I wouldn't catch so much as a whiff of any stench, the sure signal that Duke had not waited for Mommy and had already done his business (and that I would need to spend the next twenty minutes in a semi-sleepwalking state, AND totally clean out his kennel before I could go back to bed). This was always especially gross because Duke's room used to be the pantry (that's right: I built a nice, new home where I could have a big butler's pantry—that is, until I had a dog and it became the dog's room). There is a heat register in there and if the door is closed, it gets quite warm. When Duke leaves a "treat," it can really stink up the place. There is nothing like opening a door at 3:00 a.m. to a piping-hot room full of fresh shit to wake you right up! (Now, *why* didn't I buy a pet sooner?)

Assuming he did wait for me to let him out, I then had to trudge outside into the thirty-degree weather and wait for him to sniff around for the perfect spot to do his business. It was freaking cold out there, and since he was only three inches off the ground, you would think he'd want to get things over with, too, but apparently, he didn't mind hanging out for a while. So, he took his sweet time looking around (all the same places that were here the last thousand times, Duke) and I waited, trying my hardest not to face-plant, or anything, as my eyelids drooped more and more with each passing minute. But I knew (from experience) that if I didn't allow him ample time, he would punish me with a bonus bout of doggy diarrhea in the pantry, waiting for me in the morning. So I fought to keep the circulation flowing in my appendages, while Duke milled around the garden for about twenty minutes until he found the sacred ground he could pee on. Then he happily bounced back toward the door and we went back to bed.

Well, that was the plan anyway—except Duke did not want to go to sleep; now he was wide awake and ready to play. So instead of being a good dog (like they promised at the pet store), he sat in his kennel and yelped for forty-five minutes before he finally gave up and decided to rest for the remainder of the night.

Before I knew it the alarm was buzzing at 7:00 a.m.; it was time to let that damn dog out *again*! Was anyone else in my family of four going to volunteer to let him out this time? (Due to the fact that all I heard was snoring, I would have to vote "no.") Why was it my job? What if I decided to ignore the cries from the butler's pantry for once? What if Mom, heaven forbid, gave up doggy duty for a day? Then where would their precious Dukey be? So, it was on with the Uggs and out into the cold. Yet again.

It didn't take me long to figure out that these little critters also like to eat (on a regular basis). So it was a constant dance between feeding and bathroom breaks, feeding and petting, bathroom breaks and play time. It was like having another child, I tell you (except without the stretch marks, which *was* a bonus). But where to fit in a day job? Seriously, I know that there must be at least several people on the planet who get puppies and also hold down full-time jobs. How do they do it? As far as I know, you don't get maternity leave for pets, right? There is no clause for adopting a pet under the Family Leave Act is there? So then, I ask you, how do you work an eight-hour day and leave a new puppy at home when everyone knows (apparently) that they have to go to the bathroom every few hours? I had already been schooled at the pet store that you can't let a dog out alone. (Remember, major need for these guys on the black market. Hello!)

Luckily for me, my office is only a few miles from my house, because I was stopping by the house three times a day to let (my precious) Duke run around the garden and do his duty. That meant that I had to stop what I was doing (usually some kind of money-making activity that only I was capable of doing, and that only I was responsible for) so that I could drive home (wasting gas, wasting time) and let the little dog out so he could spill a whole ounce of liquid. And maybe (if I was lucky), I'd get a nugget, too, out in my flower bed. What was wrong with this picture? My day (which I used to consider to be *somewhat* important and *teetering* on successful) was now summed up in a pathetic cycle of managing doggy digestion! How did this happen?

Well, that brings us back to the present. I know the powers that be at the pet store frown on gals like me who consider ways to "off" their new dog. Now before you start dialing PETA, I don't mean "off" as in, "kill" the little guy (I am not Sarah Soprano). I mean, if Duke were to, say . . . *find a new home*, this wouldn't hurt my feelings. I guess I have a mean case of buyer's remorse, that's all. I'm envisioning my future and I want to ditch the alarm clock and work a full day and cruise my own hallway without tripping over doggy toys. I long for the way it used to be at my house: quiet, with the smell of freshly baked apple pies billowing down the stairs, instead of the scent of doggy pies. (Okay, I made that part up about the fresh baked apple pie. I have never baked a pie in my life, but it sounded better than "smell of freshly opened bags of beef jerky" or "newly unwrapped Girl Scout Cookies.")

Trouble is, I know that if I dare suggest to the kids that we sell the dog, then all of a sudden Duke will become their new best friend again; I, on the other hand, will be the devil. The mere hint of giving our precious Duke to another family would have a ripple effect that would far outlive the dog. He'd be the king of the house, and the family would monitor my every move to make sure that I wasn't doing anything shady with the dog. They'd probably even invest in some kind of doggy ankle bracelet so they would know where he was at all times. Then, if he strayed too far off our property, an alarm would go off on my daughter's backpack, or something, and a "code blue" would sound at the Animal Rescue Shelter—and I'd be arrested, under suspicion of committing an act of cruelty against a canine. My family might not even come to visit me in prison. They might not even send letters. Then Duke would take over my spot in bed. He'd assume my position at our dining room table. He would ride shotgun in my car. His picture would replace mine over our fireplace, and a stocking that read "Duke" would be hung by the chimney with care, come the holiday season.

Oh, I can see it so clearly now: that pint-sized piss-ball was laughing at me from his kennel in the pet store as he masterminded this whole drama; he knew it would only be a matter of time before I'd break. It was all part of his master plan to turn my family against me so that I'd look like the villain and he'd look like the cute little victim—who'd then take over the alpha position in *my* home! Oh, Duke spotted a live one, all right (the non-pet owner), as soon as I walked into that pet store. He pegged me, and I fell for it: hook, line and sinker.

Well, I've got news for you, you little thousand dollar flea bag, it ain't gonna happen! Not on my watch. *I* am the ruler of this domain, and it's going to take a lot more than some late night turds and midday work breaks from a midget doggy twerp to weasel me out of my family's good graces!

Bring it on Duke! I can keep pace with your little digestive track. I can keep up with your yelping spells at three in the morning; I can even laugh at how cute you are when you chew up my two hundred dollar shoes (there are more where those came from). You think it is so adorable, the way you bite holes in my recliner and gnaw the paint off the walls. (What's the matter Duke? Got a little lead poisoning?) There's nothing you can do that would make a loving pet owner (yes, I'm referring to myself) even consider letting another family raise you. So, you might as well get used to it. You are here to stay. Or, shall I say, *I* am here to stay, Duke (you are not getting my bed, my chair, my picture frame, or my stocking).

Well, readers, I hope you can check back with me in a few months, when things will have calmed down at our house. I expect Duke will have learned how to hold his load for a reasonable amount of time, and I won't have to be setting the alarm every night so he can relieve himself. I am certain that once he grows out of the "puppy" stage he won't be as interested in chewing up my furniture, either. I choose to have faith that the kids will hold up their end of the bargain and take *some* responsibility for the dog they begged for and promised to care for (whatever). You never know, maybe God is using Duke teach me a thing or two about responsibility as well (I'll have to get back to you on that one.) And who knows, maybe I will even bake an apple pie. There's a first for everything, right?

Day 1 (Again)

It is a normal Saturday afternoon. I'm sleeping on my son's bed, and he's lying next to me, watching cartoons: you know, quality time with mother and sweet, sweet son. Everything is going fine until he decides it's time to give mom "zerberts" (evidently, to try to wake me up). For those of you who don't have kids, zerberts occur when you press your face against someone's skin and blow really hard—hard enough to make fart-like noises.

Let me explain why this is such an issue for me. I'm lying on my back on the bed. For most of us, this is our "thin position." Lying on your back pulls your stomach very flat (as all the fat cells are subject to gravity). Typically, when I'm on my back I run my hand over my stomach to see if I can feel my hip bones and rib cage (if I can, then it's a skinny day; if I can't, then I am fat anyway, so bring on the

67

root beer floats). So, on my back I usually feel pretty good about myself (unless my husband is with me, which is another chapter). Not today!

As my son lifts my shirt to locate that prime real estate known as mommy's tummy, he lowers his face to connect so he can make his fart noises. Lower, lower . . . I feel his breath as his mouth finally touches my belly button. He needs to put a little muscle behind it now, because although his lips are on my skin, he hasn't hit any resistance yet. At this point, he digs his feet into the bed to create more leverage with his body, driving his small face deeper, deeper into the crevasse of my belly. Now his laughter is muffled by the consuming mass of my blubber (what's so freaking funny about this?). When he finally makes contact with solid body, he puckers up and begins to blow. Poor kid, he is laughing so hard at mommy's jelly-belly that he can hardly compose himself to produce a decent zerbert. The sound I should be hearing now is a cross between a fart and a squeak. But that's not what I hear. I can't hear anything, as a matter of fact. The laughing has stopped. Is he suffocating? Is he even breathing? (It is all fun and games until your own son suffocates in mommy-flesh.) All sides of his little face are hidden by the soft (I do tend to use moisturizer regularly) and cushy (I love describing my stomach as "cushy," thank you) roly-poly belly. This is not good!

This can only lead to one thing. There is only one remedy for this doughy debacle. I feel a "Day 1" coming on.

For those of you who have experienced Day 1, you know exactly what I'm talking about: Day 1 of a new diet, for real this time. I am serious, no more messing around. I'm going to stick to it. My gut has gotten out of hand, and I have the power to reverse it.

But the best part of Day 1 is that it goes hand in hand with "the day before Day 1." YES! The day before Day 1 is much like a bachelorette party. It's the last time you can enjoy life before it degenerates into a system: what you can eat, what you must do, and what you can't partake in. It's your last hurrah before you submit to the Day 1 regimen. In other words, it's an all-out free-for-all in the kitchen!

So, my moment of depression is short lived because I quickly alert myself that I get to partake in the Day-Before rituals! That is to say, eat whatever I want . . . and then eat some more, for good measure. This calls for grocery shopping (what should I bake?), and I'd better hurry because I only have a few hours left!

Off to the kitchen I go. The first thing I grab is a bag of frosted animal cookies. Yum! They really ought to put more than, like, six cookies in one of those bags. (I guess six cookies is a "serving," or something.) Next, I make myself a ham and cheese sandwich on a plain bagel. Now it's time to bring out the big guns: the Otis Spunk Meyer cookie dough. Blessed is he who invented the concept of frozen cookie dough! I turn on the oven and keep scrounging for delights. (How about a handful of M&M peanuts, a few pieces of licorice, and bag of fruit snacks to tide me over while I preheat the oven?) For a moment, life feels right again.

You see, before Day 1, you have a "hall pass" to indulge in all the things that you have to kiss goodbye on the following day. It never really dawns on you that if you just ate normally the day before, you'd be that much further ahead when you started Day 1. Maybe I could fit into my "skinny jeans" a whole day earlier. Of course, if I had that much self-control, there would be no need for Day 1 in the first place, so this is a moot point.

Knowing that tomorrow I start a new chapter, I somehow feel better about stuffing my face today with ice cream and cookie dough. Visions of a flat stomach and clear skin dance in my head as I lick orange Cheetos dust off my fingers (ironic isn't it?). Because tomorrow, I get serious. Tomorrow, my whole life changes. It is time to reclaim that figure I used to have—you know the "real" me—the thin, young, perky me that I met when I was seventeen, and who died when I had children. Time to call that goddess out of retirement, boys and girls.

Fast forward to the morning of Day 1. The first thing I do is survey the damage. I look at myself in the mirror before I get in the shower. First, I look head-on (not pretty), then I turn to the side (not much better), suck in my stomach (oh-oh, it is sucked in) and stand up straight. Hmmm, maybe if I stand on my tippy toes that will somehow make me look thinner (it's worth a try). Okay, well at least I have a starting point now. At least I know what I look like on Day 1, and I know I'll never look like this again. Let's go weigh in!

I can see the scale over in the corner, taunting me. It's okay to get on it the morning of Day 1 because I know it's obviously not accurate anyway. It has been at least ten pounds off since the day I got it, but I choose to humor myself. It goes without saying that I make sure I don't have any clothes or jewelry on, and no hair clips to skew the numbers while I'm on the scale (and of course I went to the bathroom first, duh!). And there it is, in black-and-white, how much I *don't* really weigh; but this cheap scale is giving me a ball park figure to be aware of as I start my new regime.

It's about this time that my stomach starts to growl. It is breakfast time. Breakfast on Day 1 is key (everyone knows you need to eat to kick-start your metabolism), so I want to make sure that I eat something that is satisfying and that will make me shit (a lot). So, I choose a glass of Fibercon and oatmeal. This is not so bad, right? I'm off to a good start. In a moment of weakness I contemplate rewarding myself with a quick handful of Hot Tamales (there is zero fat in Hot Tamales, I'll have you know), but I digress. Nothing tastes as good as thin feels, right? Whatever.

Throughout the day I do very well. I even consider that I can keep this up for an extended length of time. I have a sensible lunch, and I'm not overly hungry. My body seems to be responding well to the adjustment of caloric intake. It has been a successful Day 1 (not that I didn't toy with the idea of treating myself to an ice cream nightcap).

Before bed I find myself back in front of the mirror to check my progress. Surely I've lost five pounds or so today, right? Then I pose in front of the full-length mirror for awhile, checking my reflection in all our other mirrors until I find one that works for me. Ah, yes. I swear my ass looks a little smaller tonight (as it should), and I feel victorious. (Should I try on my skinny jeans now, or wait until tomorrow?)

While preparing for bed, I formulate my plan of attack for Day 2—which usually includes some kind of exercise. Someone once told me that in order to "lose weight and keep it off," you have to manage healthy eating habits AND consistent exercise. (By the way, haven't we invented something better than that yet? I mean, if we can take old, moldy bread and turn it into penicillin, can't we find an alternative to exercise for burning calories?) I decide to go on a walk for Day 2 (at this rate I will be a size zero before Christmas, my friend), *and* I'll allow myself one treat (don't want my body to go into detox-shock, or anything).

"Goodnight, Skinny self!" I say with a wink as I climb into bed.

Now, how long I stick to this diet usually depends on several factors:

1. Am I going on vacation anytime soon?

If the answer is yes, then my diet will normally last until I board the airplane. You see, I usually grasp the reality of my weight about five days prior to having to sport a bikini in public, so I advance into panic mode, followed by "the day before Day 1" ritual, and that leaves me three days of an actual diet before I realize that it's too late: I am already too far off the "appropriate for swimwear" radar.

2. Do I have a Fat Buddy?

This is someone who feels as disgusting and desperate as I do and has agreed to start Day 1 with me; and this time, we both promise to stick to it (no matter what). This scenario usually lasts seven to fifteen days, depending on whether one of us can actually see results. If we do, then we hang in there a little longer until one of us can break down the will power of the other and we both end up pouting over a pint of *Häagen-Dazs* and a sappy girlie movie.

3. Do I morph into Denial Mode?

This is when I am in the middle of a new diet, say, Day 5 or 6, and I have not seen any results. I have tried on all my "skinny clothes" (just to see if they're still too tight), and I have not lost a pound. At this point I determine that dieting is overrated and not worth the hassle (I mean, if I can't enjoy a doughnut from time to time without feeling guilty, then I don't want any part of it, sister). So I proceed into Denial Mode, where I conclude that I'm really not *that* fat. After all, it's not as though little kids are making fun of me on the street, or anything. I start comparing myself to real people like Rosie O'Donnell (never met a doughnut she didn't like) and Oprah (totally successful and rich), instead of Nicole Richie (anorexic) or Mischa Barton (waif). Then all of a sudden I feel better about the fact that I'm totally failing at my diet. So I bag it, and make up for lost time with some *Doritos*. It really isn't that bad being fat.

As for this particular diet sequence, I am not sure how it will end. It's almost time for me to go to bed and rise again for the (almost as familiar) Day 2. For now, I will resolve to believe the fact that my zerbert days are numbered—as I have (again) successfully made it through Day 1. And that, ladies and gentlemen, is cause for celebration, don't you think?

'Tis the Season for the Gym

Okay, it is that time I guess. We are at that point in the book where I feel comfortable sharing some things with you. I feel like we are friends now (right?), and I can share some of my not-so-fine moments with you.

I have to say that I really look forward to the fall season. So many changes are taking place outside, the leaves are turning, and the wind gets that familiar chill to it. The sun sets earlier in the day, and the kids are back in school (hallelujah). All this, of course, points to one particular thing . . . it is officially "time" to put away the bikini (assuming that you had the audacity to sport one over the summer, that is) and get out the warm, fuzzy (flab-hiding) sweaters. That's right! Turn your daisy dukes in for a nice pair of Uggs. Fall is my kind of season.

Usually during this time of the year I start to feel pretty good about myself. It becomes easier to hide the "muffin top" with a full coat than with a baby-T. If I do, however, feel like there is too much of me to love, then I typically find a friend who is sick and hang out at her house, drinking from her glass and borrowing her pillowcase (I will even lick her, if I have to) in my attempt to contract some of her virus, which might cause a decrease in my appetite. (Who cares if my tonsils swell for a few days? That can equate to a quick five-pound loss). And, since we are sharing secrets here, I am not ashamed to admit that I might have even scheduled my wisdom teeth to be extracted right before a vacation that would require me to slip into summer-wear. That's because all signs pointed to me not being able to chew for a few days, thus shedding a few unwanted pounds. (The part I was not aware of was that all I *could* eat would be ice cream, and that might really foil my plans to reach my fighting weight.)

This year, however, after a long and depressing bout with the summer "why-is-my-ass-so-big" blues (why not attempt change, the old fashioned way?), I decided it was time to join the fitness club (most people get this inkling in April or May; I guess I didn't check my messages in time). The nice thing about joining the fitness club in September is that it is pretty much isolated. I think it gets crowded between January 1st (everyone has the same New Year's Resolution, apparently) and July (most people figure that if they have not lost weight by July, then why bother since the rain is coming, anyway). So for me, September is the perfect time to begin the other "Day 1," which is Day 1 at the gym.

It is important to make a good decision before you join a gym. Most of them have sign-up fees, membership fees, and initiation fees (they figure they'd better "front load" all the fees, because they know that you won't be back after your first three weeks, anyway), so you want to choose wisely. That's my MO. After deciding to commit to some kind of regular workout, I want to make sure it's the "right" one for me, one that my (screwed-up metabolism) body will respond to (can I lose ten pounds in ten days?). So, I had begun to do some research (stall) before actually pulling the trigger on the whole gym routine.

Now I should confess, I did not actually *go out and try* several facilities before making my decision. That might be the obvious thing to do, but that sounds like a lot of work to me. My research pretty much went like this:

> SARAH: "I heard you mention you were at the gym. Which one do you go to?"
>
> LISA: "I go to Quick Fit. It's one of those 30-Second Circuit places."
>
> SARAH: "Do you even break a sweat in those places?"
>
> LISA: "Oh yes, it's a work out."
>
> SARAH: "Have you lost any weight?"
>
> LISA: "Ten pounds."
>
> SARAH: "How long did it take?"
>
> LISA: "Not long."
>
> SARAH: "I'm in."

There you have it. If Lisa could lose ten pounds (decent amount) in a short amount of time (key word: quickly) by working out for thirty minutes at a time (how easy is that?), then so could I. The very next day I drove myself right down to the facility and checked myself in (sounds like rehab, doesn't it?) for the program. (Now I really did not want to work out that day, so I signed up and then made an appointment to come back the next day to "start." Baby steps.)

My initial appointment was set for 11:30 a.m. the next day. and I was going to go with my sister-in-law who also wanted to "tone" up. I will stop right here and point out that she was there to "tone" and I was there to "lose." I should have recognized right off the bat that we were not evenly matched. She had nothing to lose; she just felt like she wanted to tone up her already tiny and perfect physique. Who does that? Mark my words, if I ever get past the "lose" category (God willing) and into the "tone" zone, I promise to be happy with what I have and go eat an Oreo.

So, the morning of the big day (Day 1 at the Gym), I stood in my closet trying to find the perfect outfit. Needless to say, the workout clothes were not exactly on the top of the pile in the ole gal's closet, if you know what I mean. I not only had to dig out some workout-wear. but I had to try it all on to see if it still fit me (from the last Day 1). Some of the items did fit (others were a gross testament to the obvious fact that I had *not* been counting calories all summer), but even these were out of style. Rule number one: if you are going to suffer the humiliation of Day 1 at the Gym, you need to at least look cute doing it. That way, the super-fit ladies who are there will feel like they have something to talk to you about (since you obviously don't have anything else in common, other than your regard for trendy fitness wear). I decided on an outfit, grabbed a power bar (that is to say, dug one out from the bottom of the "snack drawer" in the kitchen) along with a water bottle, and I hit the road.

Joan, my sister-in-law, and I decided to ride together this time (that might have been her way of making sure I got there, not sure about that), so we met at the office and took her car to the gym.

When we got there we were greeted by a cute (in a gangly sort of way) woman with a big smile. I could tell by the way she looked at me that she felt it was her duty to "save me," or something. She coddled me like it was my first day of kindergarten. She must have assumed that I hadn't spent much time (if any) in a gym prior to this encounter. Speaking loudly (as if I didn't understand "gym lingo"), she showed us both the layout of the building. Part of the policy for this place was to walk new clients through the circuit for the first few times, in case they had any questions. They also wanted to show us how to use the machines properly (because I *obviously* wouldn't know) and to make sure that our heart rate did not rev up too fast while we worked out.

As I looked around the room I could see a few ladies doing "the circuit." It was just as I had suspected. The ladies were mainly of the "mature variety," and they were smiling. They barely looked as though they were sweating at all. I was hoping for a good workout, something that made me feel like I'd accomplished something that day (so I could celebrate with a Butterfinger and not feel guilty). But I could tell that we were going to bust through this circuit and not even wipe our brow.

I got on the first machine. The owner of the gym would be my "guide" for this half hour, and the tall gangly gym attendant would be assisting Joan. The first machine was a treadmill that worked with your own foot movement. There was no on / off button, and you controlled the pace by walking or running at your desired speed. Since it was my first day, I didn't want to overdo it, but I didn't want to look like an idiot, either. If Grandma over there could pull off a run, then so I could I, right? So I ran.

Before I knew it, it was time to change stations. That first 30 seconds went by so fast that I barely had time to get in a groove (this thing was a piece of cake). *I hope this actually works*, I thought to myself. Third station, fourth station, I was working hard and trying to get my heart rate up by moving quickly from station to station, doing as many reps as I could at each one.

Ten stations down, it was time to check my heart rate. Holy Moley, I was running at a cool 25-beats-per-minute, which was optimum for weight loss (according to the chart on the wall). This wasn't so bad. I'd been here for five minutes, done ten stations, and I was in full-bore "weight loss mode." *I CAN DO THIS!* (Maybe I'd go home and try on my skinny jeans!)

Twelve, thirteen, then fifteen stations—now I was noticing something: I was not moving as quickly as I had at first. I was breathing hard and having difficulty talking. I checked out Joan, who was one station behind me (praying that she, at least, had a bead of sweat forming so I wouldn't look like a total idiot), and she, too, was beginning to tire.

Twenty stations down, I was a third of the way done, and I could really sense my vision fading in and out. My ears were popping and my boobs were sweating (not a good visual). I could see Grandma ahead of me, and she looked radiant (was she freaking singing?) and comfortable. She even gave me the "nod." You know, the nod. Like she is thinking, "Oh isn't that cute. Look at that young girl out doing something productive and good for her body." (She'd better not even give me the "atta girl, hang in there" smirk.)

Thirty stations. I needed water, now. My heart rate was holding steady at twenty-five, but my muscles were beginning to check out on me. My arms felt like limp noodles and my thighs were on fire (I didn't even remember a station that had worked my thigh muscles). Joan looked like she was beginning to suffer, as well. Her pace had slowed, and she had a mixed look of pain and sheer determination and will (Grandma must have given her the smirk).

Forty stations. Okay, this was not fun anymore. The only thing keeping me on this freaking circuit was that I was being monitored by Big Brother as he adjusted my weights and cheered me through the circuit. If I faked like I had to go to the bathroom, I knew he would make me pick up where I left off, so that was no use. If I started dragging too much, he would think I was a total wimp, so that was out. I really had only one choice, which was to continue through seven more stations until this was over.

Forty-five stations down, I could feel pearls of hard-earned sweat dripping down my back and soaking the waist of my cotton shorts. I could only hear out of my left ear, and I was not making eye contact with anyone at this point. The music was playing, but all I was listening for was the overhead voice saying "change stations" so that I could get off this roller coaster and go home.

The last station was the worst: sit-ups. I had fully intended to lie there and rest at this point, but Skippy the Gym Manager was hanging over me, all ready to count them for me (what a guy), so I had to grin and bear it for the last thirty seconds. He was trying to talk to me, at least that's what I gathered from the fact that I could see his lips moving, but all I could hear was the thumping of my heartbeat inside my head (I very well might have passed out if I'd had to get up at this point).

Finally it was over. I looked over at Joan, who was just finishing her sit-ups, and I could tell that she was beat, as well. We both pretended that we felt "great" and were eager to "do it again" as we guzzled water and limped out the door.

Once we were in the car, things got worse. I asked her how she felt, and she admitted that she was feeling a little woozy. That was an understatement. I *felt* like I'd just run a marathon in thirty minutes, and she *looked* like she had. The problem was that we'd met at the office to ride to the gym together. I was not about to attempt going back to work, and I was in no condition to get behind the wheel, either. At the risk of sounding like a completely out-of-shape, pathetically exhausted gym partner, I told Joan that she had to drive me home because I couldn't physically drive myself. I literally felt like I could chuck my power bar at any moment, and I knew I needed to lie down. (Plus, it was time for my favorite soap. Bonus!).

Joan obliged my request and dropped me at my front door. We barely had the energy to make eye contact and enunciate our words fully. She muttered a few things that I was still trying to translate as she pulled away. I was pretty sure she'd told me that she needed to "call it a day," and that she hoped I would feel better soon.

I crawled inside the house and onto the welcoming couch. I laid there in all my glory and tried to think about the positive things, as I flipped through the channels. I tried to focus on the fact that, at least, I *went* to the gym ("A" for effort) and *attempted* a full-body workout (at least, I had lived to tell the tale). I tried to think of things I loved about myself like, I am funny, I am smart, and I have lots of killer shoes. But everyone knows that *fat* people like to buy shoes. These are the only things that remain constant when your ever-changing waistline is busting (no one ever lies about their shoe size). Okay, back to the positives . . . I have pretty thick hair, which is easy to style (but apparently, I am the triple threat, because with thick hair comes a thick waist and ankles). I have nicely manicured nails (well I did, but I quit going to the nail salon because I knew all the skinny bitches that worked there were talking about my fat ass in some other language, while I slumped at their manicure station).

Obviously this little exercise in self-affirmation was not working. (Hey, did I say "exercise?" Does that count?) It was time for me to hit the fridge, grab my *Star Magazine*, and find some unfortunate rich celebrities to make fun of. They may be skinny, but I wouldn't want the rest of the emotional baggage they have to deal with.

What was this? Lo and behold, on the front cover of my rag-mag was a huge caption, reading: "How the Stars Get Thin"! HELLO! Now they were speaking a language I could understand. I quickly flipped through the pages until I found the article (obviously a sign from God). The article told all about how celebs got this "wonder pill" from their publicists and other industry insiders on the Q.T. So, I read on, trying to find a name, a website, some way that I could find the pill. (Apparently, the gym is overrated. I knew it.) I found the website URL and practically tripped myself running from the couch to my computer (energy was back in full swing, I guess). I decided to ignore the rest of the article that concluded how bad this pill was for you (show me the proof), and how it was supposed to be some kind of medication for dying horses (sometimes I feel like a horse), and how there were severe side effects (you say tomato, I say tomaaahto), and also that it was illegal (worth a risk, baby, worth a risk).

I was rummaging through my wallet to get the credit card out when the website finally came up on the screen. Scroll down, scroll down . . . desperate to find a link to shop online, I realized for a fleeting nanosecond that I was acting a bit ridiculous. I mean, if anyone were to walk in and see me ordering horse drugs in an attempt to shed twenty pounds, this would not be my finest moment. But, I would risk it (I said "fleeting").

And as quickly as my energy peaked, it crashed, just like that. Staring at my computer, I felt all the excitement being sucked out of me, as I realized that I would likely have to return to Quick Fit, yet another day. The illegal horse pill had been blacklisted. It was "unavailable." No go, *amigo*! No dice. Not in this lifetime, sister. Shit!

So, I have made a decision. I will go back to the gym and try again (someday). Maybe it won't be so bad next time. Maybe I will even get to the place where I am comfortable and confident in my own skin. Maybe I will stop focusing on the scale for five minutes, and enjoy a workout, because it is good for my health and my spirit. But for now, I will relax with a bowl of ice cream and figure out what I would have to do to merit my very own publicist.

Break-out on the High Seas

I may or may not have mentioned up until this point that I am happily involved in a direct sales company that specializes in natural-based spa products (a.k.a. skin care). That is correct: I got on the direct sales bandwagon and rode, baby, like a bandit on his way out of town. Selling skin care in your thirties has its advantages, as you might guess. I am already blessed with good skin, and still being relatively young as well, so that's a double whammy. Put me in front of a bunch of hopefuls and they get ready to write the kind of checks you only read about. You might say that I embody the epitome of all that is possible with just an ounce of help from natural mango oil, a pinch of sea kelp extract, and a little quality time in the shower with an exfoliator! At least I used to.

When I mention that I am happily involved with this company, I should tell you that I am *really* involved. I am at the top of the company (hold your applause until the end), which means that I earn many great trips to exotic places. (Is this beginning to sound like a recruiting commercial?) The best part of my business is that I get to choose my own hours. (Okay, I just threw that one in to entertain all my direct sales sisters who are reading this!) In one particular year, I earned a trip to Mexico aboard a luxury cruise liner. My husband, Brian, and I were really excited because he had never been on a cruise before, and we'd be anchoring at ports we had never had the opportunity to explore.

(It goes without saying that my pre-cruise ritual consisted of dieting, shopping, finding babysitters for the kids, then more dieting and even a little self-starvation. But, if you need more graphic details of this account, refer back to a previous chapter; I am sure it's a repeat performance of former diet angst.)

Finally, the big day arrived: we were to fly to Florida to get ready for our big adventure aboard the "Jewel of the Sea." Once there, we grew more excited as the other incentive achievers met in the hotel lobby and hugged and kissed each other and played little games of catch-up, while we waited to be bused to the luxury vessel. So far so good: I had cute new sunglasses on, a great spray tan, and I was surrounded by some of my dearest skin care colleagues and friends. Ahoy, Mate!

One day into the voyage, I noticed something unsightly growing on my forehead. It was not a zit. (I repeat: it was *not* a zit. I knew this because *I did not get zits*. Ask anyone.) Strange, though it was, I treated it like a zit and immediately doused it with a cocktail of zit zappers and cover-up. I assumed that it was flying solo, and I left my cabin with high hopes that it would have landed elsewhere by the time I looked in the mirror again next morning.

Not so. By the next day, my friendly little blemish (I only say blemish for your benefit because they have not come up with a word to accurately describe something that *resembles* a zit, but is surely *not* a zit—because, remember, I do not get zits), and this friendly little blemish had enlisted the help of a little buddy to get my attention. Now I had two (non-zits) on my forehead and wasn't sure what to do about it. I mean, after all, I was there representing a skin care company; how would it look if one of the top performers had broken out like a teenaged girl? (I could see the stock prices plummeting.)

Since my zit zapper had failed me, I needed to try something else. The problem was that I didn't have a lot of experience in this area (you understand), so I didn't know how to battle these things. I decided that Neosporin would be my best line of defense. My cognitive thinking skills told me that zits are caused by bacteria; bacteria signify infection. Therefore, Neosporin would be good for zits. So, I lubed my forehead up like a Butterball Turkey and went to lie in the sun. (For those of you who have experienced instant acne, you already feel my pain and know where this is going.)

I don't know how much time passed that day. I don't know what was happening inside my body or on the surface of my skin for my face to be transformed the way it was; but when I went back to my cabin that afternoon, I must have had a minimum of 300 little (non-zit) red bumps in residency on my forehead. There was no way that a dab of zit zapper or a smear Neosporin was going to help me at this point. I was in big, big, red and oozing trouble!

I want you guys to have the full benefit of reliving this nightmare with me, so I am going to share a few details with you that I forgot to mention. On this cruise I needed to do many things: be video-taped for an upcoming training video, promote our product line to strangers, share my "expertise" with aspiring leaders within our organization, and also pose for countless photo-ops with reps, Home Office staff—and let's not forget the company CEO. And there I was with a forehead that looked like ground hamburger. The more I tried to camouflage it with make-up, the worse it looked. The more I tried to pick it, pop it, squeeze it or mangle it, the worse my condition grew, and the more those bumps multiplied. It was if my condition had a mind of its own, and if I tried to feed it something it didn't like, instead of puking it up or shedding it like bodyweight, as normal people would, it hoarded its unknown toxins, mutating into a stronger, more resistant version of itself just to spite me.

Everyone I knew on the trip offered advice about how to treat it (bless their hearts). Each person, it seemed, had his or her own remedy for my condition. I got all kinds of advice: from taking vitamins to drinking special tea. I tried almost every kind of over the counter medication (no matter what it was for) and even some that were not so "over the counter" (if you catch my drift). Nothing worked. Desperate to reclaim my beauty, I tested some of the more peculiar suggestions as well. For example, one gal mentioned her Great Aunt Esther had once told her to apply toothpaste (seems harmless enough), then pour cough syrup over that (if you say so, sister), and then sleep facing the moon—while holding a dragonfly in your left hand (okay, now you lost me). Another friend suggested that I paint my face with peanut butter and then bake in the sun. The oil from the peanut butter was supposed to neutralize the yeast that was likely causing the break-out, and the sun was supposed to "dry it out." No, it was more like this instead: the oil from the peanut butter clogged the rest of my pores, and the sun made me smell like a fresh-baked peanut butter cookie!

Then there was the *other* type of advice. (This is precious.) This came from my sisters, who were also on the trip. (Haven't you ever heard the old saying, The family that sells skin care together, stays together?)

"Sarah, just leave it alone. Don't touch it," they told me.

Yeah, okay! I thought to myself. *You try that.* First of all, it freaking hurt, okay? My face was on fire. It felt like I'd been carved up with a serrated knife. My skin was dry and irritated, tight and red. And the pearl of wisdom they came up with was to *leave it alone*? (Why didn't I think of that?)

One of the highlights of the trip came when I was talking to a younger gal who was sitting next to me during our free time. She wasn't involved with my company; she was a guest on the cruise with her family. Normally, I'm really outgoing and I meet lots of new people on these kinds of trips, but I had kept to myself more than usual on this one (go figure). I did, however, manage to have a conversation with this particular gal out on the deck toward the end of our high seas adventure. She was a nice gal, about my age, and we seemed to connect right away. We talked about life, kids, and work. The subject of what I did came up, as well as why I was on the "free" trip. I explained to her a little about my company and what I did. (It is important to note that, normally, this would be a good thing. She would be intrigued by the fact that I was involved in a company that provided their representatives the opportunity to earn free travel, and I would tell her all about it and how she, too, might want to consider this business opportunity. Textbook recruiting stuff, you guys.)

I will never forget the look on her face. She looked at me, raised her sunglasses and rested them on top of her head, then said, "Sarah, do *you* use Sensaria?" Classic!

My skin looked like that for the entire trip. There was nothing I could do. The more remedies I tried, the worse my condition grew. Even two weeks after I returned home my forehead had that raw hamburger look.

I am happy to report that it has not recurred since. To this day, I don't know what caused that "break-out," but I sure know that I never want an encore. One thing I learned about myself on that trip is that I was really the only one who was obsessed about my face. I was still the same person on the inside. My unsightly forehead didn't take away from the fact that I was a great representative for the company, a great friend or a loving wife. We still managed to have a blast on the cruise. *I* was the one who was continually pointing out my flaws to everyone, as if they even cared.

I thought about including a photo from that trip in this book so that you could see how bad it was (God knows, there were sure enough of them taken), but then I decided against it. I am choosing instead to view this chapter as closure. This is me, turning the proverbial page, if you will, on the nightmare I endured on the high seas; as you should, too. Go on, turn the page, and put this visual of me in all my break-out glory behind you, never to return again.

10

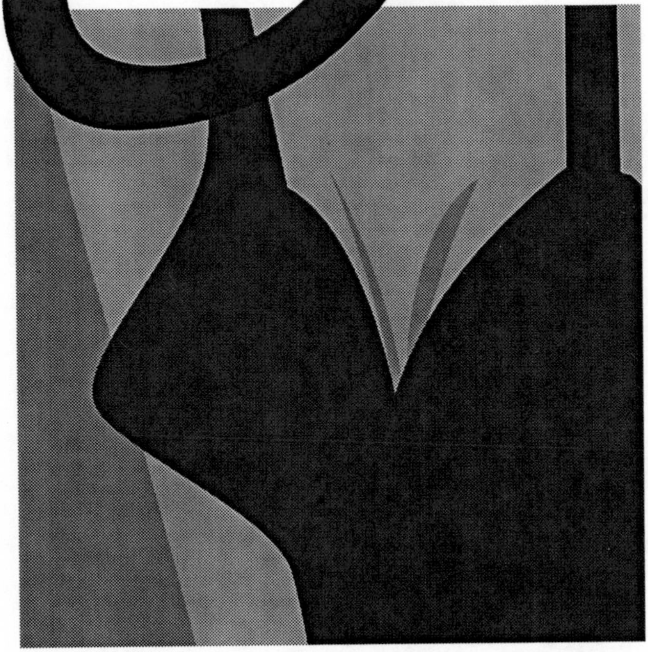

High on Life

Since I had never done it, I decided to climb a mountain on my 31st birthday. It is never too late to begin, right? What better way to celebrate my adulthood (prove that I'm not a wimp) and become one with nature (whatever) than to brave the beast herself. After all, how hard can it be? But before you go getting too impressed with me, let me confess something: I am from Washington State, and when we use the term *mountain*, I think snow-capped ski slopes at four thousand feet. In Arizona, however, mountains are really nothing but overgrown (and overrated) piles of dirt that have yet to be bought up by some over-zealous land developer. So when my friend Erica asked me to hike to the top of Camel Back *Mountain*, I did not want to point out the obvious (so as not to embarrass her) and just agreed that it would be a fun "walk in the park" (if you know what I mean).

In hindsight, I can say that I would have probably fared better if I had slept the night before, enjoyed some kind of sustenance the morning of, or had access to even a drop of water during our adventure. I guess that's where a little experience would have been nice (or even an inkling of knowledge about the great outdoors).

If I would have had a diary with me (access to a pen, and my wits about me), my entries from that day might have read something like this:

Off I go. At first, the hike seems pretty easy. Lots of "rock stairs" to assist my climb. There is a nice path to follow and mile markers, too, so you know where you are. I can see the top . . . doesn't seem that far. Oh look, there's a golf course, and a pool, and there is the cityscape. The view's not bad from 250 feet. (*At this point I am still feeling pretty good about myself and my chances of survival. I am not really tired yet, and my body is still responding in harmony to the signals given by my central nervous system. So life is good.*)

I press on. Now, the path looks a little less traveled. I can't make it out as clearly. The rock stairs are gone, and now I am forced to find my own way to climb. (*At this point in the journey I begin to wonder if I remembered to tell anyone where I was going. And why didn't anyone remind me to bring a carabineer? I'm struggling with the fact that I have no idea what I'm doing, and when faced with the alternatives of continuing the ascent or turning around and going back down, neither option looks very alluring.*)

Okay, now this is beginning to get ridiculous. Where is the damn trail? Where are the mile markers? Do I have to rely on instinct to reach the summit? Shouldn't I be to the top by now? And I haven't seen the water cart come by. (*It goes without saying that I don't have a plethora of survival skills to draw from, so it's slim pickings as far as exit strategies for me. Things are not looking good.)*

Now it turns on me. This is no longer a leisurely day hike to the top of a dirty hill; this is an actual mountain climb that demands my respect. *(I'd like to respectfully decline to go any further.)* Each movement has to be calculated so that I don't plunge over the edge. And what if my hand slips as I try to haul myself up and over the gritty face of this huge basalt formation? Dragged across jagged rock with every lift, my body aches. All my muscles stall and quiver; my mouth is dry and tastes of dust and red dirt. *(And let the record show that this is not an exaggeration. This sucks. My poor manicured hands are bleeding in protest, and my softly shaven legs are as scratched as my favorite Prince CD. Happy Freakin' Birthday, Sarah!)*

Daylight is waning now. I have to rely on my survival skills. I don't want to end up being the focus of an episode on the Discovery Channel—after having to saw off my own foot. As I look ahead, all I see is rock. I can't see the top; I can't see a trail; I can't see anything but the face of an unforgiving formation and a few cacti. I don't even know if I'm going the right way. All I know is that one mistake, one slip of these Nikes and I am snake bait. *(I think this entry speaks for itself. No additional commentary needed.)*

I pull and claw my way to the top. Victory! Too bad I'm working too hard to breathe to really savor my achievement. I don't know how I got here, really. Maybe it was luck. I know it's the top because I see people holding their stopwatches and checking their pulses. I see people sitting down with water bottles and cameras. I see dogs lying down and panting on the rocks. Okay, where is the guy that takes your photo and sells it to you for twenty bucks? Where is the gal selling T-shirts? And what time does the shuttle come to take me down (every half hour and on the hour?) And what's with that chipper four-year-old over there; how the heck did *he* get up here? (*What the hell is this? Did they find an alternate route up here? Is there, like, stairs or a gondola, or something that I don't know about? Because I am here to tell you that there is no way that old women and children could have braved the face of this peak the way I just did without medics on the ready!*)

As I look around, regrets flood my brain. I might have enjoyed this had I been a little more prepared. I might have done better had I stretched out before such an attempt. And I'm sure this view would seem worth it all—if I could just see through all these clouds. I might even have lingered here awhile, but it's 50 degrees. Dehydrated as I am, how can I feel good about myself when my tired and hungry brain is unable to compute the experience into anything memorable enough to warrant my decision to take on this death walk in the first place?

Okay, time to go. Let's get down! (*This, of course, would have been my last entry, because even if I had had a diary, I would've been so grumpy at this point, I'm sure I would have hurled it off a cliff about this time.*)

Now normally, you'd think that the way down would be a snap, right? I think it would be if I had real hiking shoes on (and an inkling as to what I am doing). The way down is a game of what I call "squat, step, and pray." Lower your body down, brace yourself, take a step and pray that that rock is stable. Take a step and pray that your Nikes don't slip out from under you on the loose gravel. Take a step and pray that no one takes a picture of you.

Muscles that I didn't even know I had are begging for relief. My eyes are dry and chalky as I try to navigate my way to the bottom. My hands are dirty and chafed and my fingers are swollen like little sausages. My legs feel like noodles and my head pounds in concert with my pulse. With each weighted step, my knees wince.

Finally, I reach the bottom. I know it is the bottom because it is crowded with happy-go-lucky twenty-somethings, eager to watch the sunset from the summit. (Show-offs.) They are only smiling because they have not yet realized their imminent danger. Let's see them on the way down (if they make it, that is).

Once I reach the car I know I am going to live. It is over. The soft black leather interior of a Honda Civic never felt so good. The sweet taste of a melted strawberry smoothie and a stale blueberry muffin never hit the spot like this.

I think I will stick to things I know best. I'm fine with the fact that I'm not an outdoorsman. I don't hang out at REI, don't subscribe to *Field & Stream*, don't watch the Outdoor Channel; and you won't find me at the Rocky Mountain Elk Foundation Convention. I don't have to prove anything to anybody. I am who I am. So tomorrow, I'm going shopping (just to prove it).

Lessons from the Spa

I have always been a girlie girl. I like to do girlie things like wear make-up, shop for clothes, and talk on the phone (sometimes for hours on end about absolutely nothing of any importance). What goes right along with the aforementioned girlisms is the fact that I love to go to the spa. What girl doesn't like to be pampered? There's an unspoken bond between the ladies: once you enter the big welcoming doors of the spa and you take your first whiff of the beckoning eucalyptus, you're part of the club. Life as you know it changes. You will no longer accept mediocrity. You will no longer consider your husband's half-assed backrubs and homemade coupons for "body wraps" an acceptable exchange for the real deal. Once you've tasted the sweet life at the spa, there ain't no going back, baby.

Luckily for me, I work in an industry where I'm able to visit with my spa sisters often. I have traveled a lot with my direct sales company, and I have always ensured that my accommodations included a nice spa with an appointment on their docket at some point during my stay. As you might guess, this makes for some great "spa stories"—some of which are good, some less noteworthy. I've been poked and prodded by the best of them; and I have been rubbed and flubbed by novices as well. Let me share with you a few things that happened to me on one such trip to the spa in Las Vegas.

I must preface this by saying that The Hotel houses my very favorite spa on the entire planet. If you ever get a chance to go there, you should. From the moment you walk in, you feel you are someplace really special. The first time I went, all I could think about was how I could find a way to bring twenty of my closest friends down there with me (and I did do that, by the way, about a year later). Faux suede, stone-washed fabrics, waterfalls—the modern décor gracing the lobby is beautiful.

During my first visit, I decided to go in a little early so that I could enjoy the amenities before my massage. After undressing in the locker room, I strolled out into the main area where the pools, sauna, and steam room were located. The first thing I noticed was all the beautiful (naked) women. I was not in Kansas anymore: these gals were pumped full of saline, Restylene, and Botox. There were boobs on display, tight asses at every angle, and face lifts pulled so tight that some of these gals could no longer close their mouths completely. There I was, in all my Pacific Northwest (a.k.a. "natural") beauty trying to figure out how to be modest without looking like a total prude. I decided to grab a chair close to the pool, beneath a towering ficus tree (with its glossy weeping fig leaves, which come into the story later). That way, when I dropped my towel, my lady garden would only be exposed for a nanosecond before it disappeared under the steamy waters of the pool (so as not to offend any clean-shaven vixens luxuriating nearby).

It takes a lot of skill to time that first dip just right. First, you have to scan the room. You have to make sure that no one is in clear view of you when your towel drops (at least, no one who might barf after one look at your stretch marks). Then you also have to ensure that no one is in your way: you want an unobstructed path from your chair to the stairs of the Jacuzzi so that you can quickly submerge any unsightly body parts before anyone in the vicinity notices your towel has dropped. (You are the Stealth Dipper; you must be cautious, young grasshopper.) This is twice as important when you are in Las Vegas, as imperfection is rarely *allowed* in the spa. The lady patrons there are bought and paid for, and when you're in their midst you'd better act like you're on the guest list, if you know what I mean. Act shy and demure when these gals start splashing, and you're likely to get caught in a Shelia Sandwich (if you get my drift).

However, executing the "stop, drop, and sprint" to the pool (in an attempt *not* to be noticed) is the quickest way to *be* noticed, come to find out. When everyone around you is relaxing and showing off their latest plastic surgery, being the soccer mom who is embarrassed by her stretch marks puts you in the minority.

My challenge to keep a low profile that day was foiled from the beginning. Not to worry, there were more places to hang out at the spa. Next up, the steam room!

That steam room is one of my favorite places; its eucalyptus-scented air is amazing. I hung my robe on the door outside the steam room, wrapped my towel tightly around my chest, then entered the foggy chamber. It was eerie and quiet in there. It was too quiet, actually, and so foggy that I couldn't tell if I was alone or not. I sank down on the first bench I came to and began to relax. Inhaling the sweet vapors of the aromatherapy, I melted into the steamy towel and occasionally blotted my face and neck.

A few minutes passed and the fog began to clear. I could make out silhouettes now. Several gals shared the room with me, none of whom had spoken a word (there must be an unwritten code mandating silence in the steam room, or something; I'll make a note of that). As the haze dispersed, I found myself sitting among seven perfectly proportioned model-type ladies who were *buck naked,* engaged in obvious detox from a night of hardcore partying. It seemed the reason they were not talking had more to do with the fact that their bodies were recuperating than the previously mentioned spa etiquette. I was the only one in a towel, and it was surely obvious to them that I must be hiding something (saddle bags and love handles perhaps?). So, once again, I was standing out like a sore thumb.

Not to worry, I'm a quick learner. The next day when I returned to the spa with my sister Jeni and my close friend Amy, I was eager to catch them up on the rules of the steam room. Sure, they were both a little shy at first about going commando in the fog zone with nothing between them and utter humiliation but water vapor, but I assured them that it would be worse to wear a bathing suit or a towel into the room, because that only screams "insecure," and we did not want *that* label amongst Vegas's finest. So with that, we dropped our towels (and our inhibitions) and into the steam room we fled, buck naked.

What happened here? What had changed from yesterday? Obviously, I had missed the memo. No one left a message on my phone saying Tuesdays were *not* naked days in the steam room. As the big glass door swung open to reveal the three of us in all our glory (that is to say, childbearing hips, postpartum boobs, and spare tires), it also allowed the accumulated steam to escape. So now, we were in plain view of all the ladies sitting there facing us, in what I can only assume was amazement. None of them (I repeat, *none*) were naked; just us. They were chastely trussed up in white towels, pristine as Catholic school girls, and they looked at us in utter disgust as we trooped in—like trailer trash just off the bus from the ghetto. (What happened to the hookers that were here yesterday? Where did they go? *They* made me look like Barbara Bush, for crying out loud!)

The silence was broken only by the sound of our naked butts slapping the wet tile of the steamy bench, splashing the water out of its resting place. You could have cut the tension with a knife as the patrons looked on, no doubt repulsed by the very idea of all the germs we might be dispersing. There was nowhere to hide. We were in the steam room. Naked. Everyone was starring at us. Correction, make that *me*; in addition to the primly toweled gapers, now Jeni and Amy were shooting daggers of fury toward me with their eyes. After all, I got us into this mess in the first place: I was the one who'd read them the rules of steam room etiquette, remember?

From where I was sitting, there was only one way to escape with our dignity still intact, and it was too late for that, so we needed to just get up and leave quietly. We needed to pretend that we'd meant to do this. We needed to forget this little mishap ever happened and go on our merry way and hope that none of these ladies would recognize us later (with our clothes on). So, on the count of three, we stood up and bee-lined for the door.

Houston, we have a problem.

Seems someone had run off with our robes while we were in the steam room. Nice. Now, we three *amigos* were in the hallway, naked, with nothing to cover up with and no terrycloth to be found. Guess who was (unanimously) nominated to hunt down some fig leaves (figuratively speaking) to cover ourselves. Me!

I just couldn't win for losing. I'd tried to take my friends out for a nice trip to the spa, and this was the thanks I got. Word to the wise, when heading into the steam room, *always* take a towel. Worst-case scenario, you can always use it to sit on, and you'll never get caught with your pants down when you come out.

But I hadn't given up on the spa. My final stop was the actual treatment room, where the real fun begins, ladies. On this particular day I was indulging in a massage with Matt. He came out to the waiting area to greet me, and I was immediately excited (not that kind of excited, relax). He was tall and seemed to have good hands. He said he'd been a masseur for a few years and told me he'd take good care of me (yeah, baby).

Once settled into the room, I situated myself on the table. Matt began working on my upper back, and I inhaled deep breaths of lemongrass and lavender aromatherapy. So far, so good. His pressure was a little light, but I figured it was just his warm-up technique (bless his heart). But a few minutes went by, and it still felt more like my husband's attempts to rub my back before asking for sex. Not quite sure today's session was worth my buck-o-fifty, I hoped Matt would show his *skills* any minute, because I was getting bored.

At least thirty minutes into my hour "massage" I had yet to enjoy a single moment of his pathetic display of intimacy. He was running his hands up and down my back like a blind man searching for keys on the kitchen counter (am I on candid camera?). *Should*

I say something, I wondered, *or should I just keep my mouth shut and let him finish?* I suddenly realized I was having a conversation in my head about something more reminiscent of a pitiful one night stand than a massage, AND I was going to be paying for it! Seriously, I was hoping with each passing moment that it would be over soon.

Just when I thought he was nearing the crescendo of his masterful rubdown, Matt leaned in to get a better angle on my thigh. His face was close to mine. He started panting, as if on the verge of an orgasm. He had sweat beading on his brow (I only knew this, of course, because it was dripping on my shoulder), and he was literally breathing in tandem with the kneading pulse of his hands (now this was just weird). Stranger still, I didn't feel any pressure. He looked like he had just run the freaking Boston Marathon; I, on the other hand (no pun intended), was barely firing any neuron receptors during this damn "treatment."

For the rest of the hour I could hardly keep from laughing. I actually began to feel sorry for Matt. I mean, I'm sure he meant well, but I knew he couldn't have received many good reviews from his past clients. There was no way on God's green earth that he could have drummed up *any* repeat customers.

At the end of our time together Matt looked me in the eye and asked me how I felt. He asked if I had enjoyed it (was it good for you?). I didn't know what to say. Again, this sounded more like a conversation reserved for a one night stand (as if I'd ever had one, I mean). I didn't have the courage to break his heart; I had to smile and nod. I couldn't tell him that he lacked anything even slightly resembling useful massage skills, couldn't mention that his breath reeked of Cream of Chicken soup, or that my five-year-old son had given me better foot massages. No, I did what any other

self-respecting woman—who didn't want to bruise a man's ego—
would do.

I told him it was good.

Then later, when he was gone, I went to the girls at the front
desk and complained about his performance (and got my money
back).

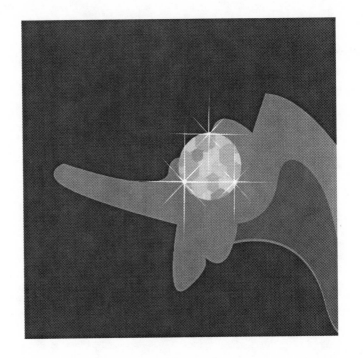

12

My (Almost) Date With a Celebrity

I never see famous people. I've traveled a lot, too, visiting places where I think I might see someone famous and then . . . nothing. The closest I've come to a run-in with someone of elite status was when I saw Conrad Bain. (Who the hell is that, you ask? He's the guy who played Mr. Drummond on *Diff'rent Strokes*.) Bain was sitting on a bench waiting for the ferry (actually, now that I think about it, *I* didn't see him; it was my Uncle who saw him and then told me about it later that day).

I already told you that when I went to L.A. last time and camped my ass on Rodeo Drive (in hopes of peeping some celeb in search of some fashion must-haves), I did not see a single A-lister (or even a B-lister, for that matter). In all my travels, airport after airport, you would think I'd have run into *someone*. Nope.

But my friends, who never go anywhere, always seem to run into the famous. It never fails. One friend, who's a total homebody and never leaves the comfort of her little town, might venture out (for once) to Las Vegas, for example. No sooner does she step off the freaking plane and she is texting me that she's walking to baggage claim behind Shaquille O'Neal. But the fun doesn't stop there because before her weekend is over, she has rubbed elbows with Matt Damon at the poker table at the Bellagio (I can't tell you how many times I've been there), sipped cocktails with David Spade at the Mirage (who does that?), and exchanged beauty secrets with Jenny McCarthy, poolside at the Mandalay Bay (whatever)!

I, on the other hand, go to Las Vegas *all the time*. The closest I come to eyeing the rich and famous is seeing a few "up and comers" at the Comedy Stop at the Trop, after shelling out seventeen bucks a head! Similarly, when I land at LAX, I always seem to be a day late or a week early. Oh, I read about how the celebs were just cruising through the airport "moments" prior to my arrival (signing autographs and kissing babies, no doubt) but when I'm there, the coast is pretty freaking clear.

All this bitching is prelude to the fact that when I took my most recent trip to California, I used a different approach. I decided to attract abundance in my life (in all areas), starting with my attitude about my vacation. On the flight down south I decided that I would "see some celebrities this time, for sure." (Why does this even matter to me? I'm not sure about this, but for the sake of this chapter, just go with it) So, I declared it. I laid the foundation for a great week of celeb sightings (and whatever else people do while in California).

After all this build up, you would think that I was about to tell you an amazing story about how my life was forever changed by my chance meeting with Brad Pitt, or my crazy girls-night-out with Madonna or something, right? Well, not quite the case here. But the good news is, I did (finally) see a real-life celebrity. That's the cool part of the story. It was Vince Vaughn. He (at the time of this publishing anyway) is an A-list actor, and I am a big fan. He has headlined some of my favorite movies (sure to be cinematic classics), and I was excited that he was my "first" (totally trumps Conrad Bain, anyway). But the whole story (don't worry, I'm getting to it) is less than impressive; in fact, it kind of pisses me off when I think about it. Let me explain.

Brian, my sister-in-law, brother-in-law, and I all decided to take a trip to California in February to celebrate my birthday (week) and catch a little bit of sunshine after several weeks of Seattle rain (shocker). We didn't have a hotel reservation (or even an inkling of a plan, for that matter). All we knew was that we'd fly into Santa Barbara and fly out of San Diego at the end of the week. It would be an adventure of sorts, the four of us hanging out, looking for good seafood, sunshine, a nice golf course and, of course, celebrities (I think Joan and I were the only ones with much interest in people watching, and this definitely played into the decision to head to southern California.) The only plan I really made ahead of time was securing the rental car. This turned out to be a little bit of a feat in itself because, apparently, if you want to pick a car up in one locale and drop it off in a different one, that's an issue. So of course, the rental car companies reserve the *special* cars (think sleds) for customers with this particular request. (You can imagine that we felt like "high society" rolling around Malibu in a 1999 Mercury Grand Marquis.)

The four of us ended up staying at a great hotel resort called the Bacara Hotel and Spa in Santa Barbara that first night. It nestled oceanside, right on a cliff. There were panoramic views of the sea from every room (well, *almost* every room, as we would find out). We hung out, toured the grounds, went to the indoor gym (why, I wonder) and got massages at the spa. The real fun began when we decided to hit the bistro for dinner at about nine o'clock, after the massages. Joan and I were too tired to really "get ready," so we decided to go to dinner in "resort casual" mode (ball caps, yoga pants, flip flops—oh, and no make-up). When we walked in with our husbands, it seemed to be a nice place but few diners were present (we must have missed the rush). A total of two tables were occupied in the entire restaurant, and the hostess, bless her heart, seated us right next to one of them. So, a whole roomful of empty tables to choose from and she sits us next to a table taken by two guys. For a minute, I thought about complaining (easy, Trigger), but I decided to go with the flow and not make an issue out of it.

As I sat down, I glanced at the men at the next table. *That looks like Vince Vaughn,* I thought to myself. *Holy shit, it is Vince Vaughn. A real-life celeb, sitting right next to me! Hallelujah! (Where's my flipping camera phone?) Buckle up ladies and gentlemen; we're in for a fun night.* This guy is a genuine kick in the pants, and he was sitting just three feet from us for the duration of our meal. Did it get any better than this? It was like having a front row seat at a comedy club without having to pay for it. I wondered if he'd dish top-secret plans for his new movie. I couldn't wait to sneak into the bathroom and text my sister back home (but I didn't want to risk missing him glance at me or say something funny).

Just then it dawned on me: I hadn't taken a shower; I looked like death. I couldn't have looked worse had I just crawled out of bed, endured a high impact aerobics class (not that I'd ever actually sported that look) and headed straight down to the bistro. Nice! I determined it was worth missing a few one-liners to roll some gloss over my lips (and make sure there were no unsightly poppy seeds caught in my teeth), so I made a quick trip to the bathroom before any of the real action began.

You'll remember that we'd arrived at the bistro at about eight thirty and were immediately seated. You'll also recall that there weren't many people there. Well, we left the restaurant at about ten forty-five. Was this because we were holding court with V.V. and his posse, laughing, drinking, and carrying on? Nope. Was it because we were savoring a nice five-course meal, letting it digest and then cleansing our palate with gourmet coffee and an after-dinner mint? Not so. Well then, why on God's green earth did we spend over two hours in that bistro with all of ten other patrons on a Tuesday night in February, you ask? Because each of the ten waiters on staff that night had their head so far up Vince Vaughn's ass, we couldn't even get so much as a pat of butter brought to our table with our first request.

Upon arrival, our waiter must have mentally put us on *ignore* for the first twenty minutes as he scurried about, making sure that Mr. Vaughn and company had a plethora of tasty delights littering their table. Cocktails, an overflowing bread basket, a few open bottles of San Pellegrino—they had it all, even before their asses hit the chairs; whereas we had already taken a bathroom break before we even had menus in hand (hardly what I'd had in mind when craving a close encounter with a celeb).

Once we finally did get the attention of our *garçon*, he couldn't even run through the specials for us without looking over my husband's shoulder to catch a better view of Vince. Obviously, our waiter was trying to anticipate any needs the resident "star" might have (an ass wiping, perhaps) and wasn't even listening to us as we asked for his recommendations for the evening. And I have to tell you that this bistro was not cheap (yes, I'll have a hard-boiled egg on a bed of Hamiltons, please). So we were definitely paying for the service (to say the least). Well, according to the brochure, this little haunt claimed to have the trifecta of the best service, the best atmosphere, and the best food on the entire property.

I already told you that the service was going south in a New York minute. Although these guys were staffed at a three-to-one ratio, you wouldn't know it because all eyes were on the tall dude at Table Three. I swear that all the wait staff was in the kitchen playing a gnarly game of rock-paper-scissors—just for the chance to fill a water glass or fold the napkin of V.V. roughly every fifteen seconds. Meanwhile, the four of us (nobodies) at the adjacent table were doing nothing but cramping their style with our hunger pangs and outlandish requests for futile things like utensils and condiments.

When we finally did get someone's attention long enough to order our entrées, it took our food forty-five minutes to arrive tableside. And in the interim, you'd think the staff would be filling our drinks and apologizing for the delays. No dice. They were busy making arrangements for Vince's anticipated departure. ("Would you like a cart to escort you back to your villa, Mr. Vaughn? Would you like a male or female driver? Would you like a black cart or a white cart? Would you prefer it to have a full tank of gas or a half tank of gas, Mr. Vaughn?")

The atmosphere, on the other hand, was nothing to scoff at. Well, that's what the brochure had promised. I would not be able to testify to this firsthand because it was dark when we arrived, plus, my senses went pretty much numb after about ten minutes (due to lack of nutrients to the brain, plus, I am also pretty sure my core body temperature dipped below the safety zone a few times while inside). Huge doors opened onto the dining patio, which allowed for a nice view of the ocean and the flickering lights of the tiki torches (and also allowed for those gale-force winds blowing through to our table to complete the ambience). It was so freaking cold in there that I petitioned the waiter to close the doors to the patio. Clearly, the restaurant was mostly empty. Except for the tumbleweed blowing through at warp speed, nothing was coming in and out of those doors (I was pretty sure that even our boy Vinny would be catching a chill had they not loaded him up with hot coffee and hand warmers). The waiter declined my request, stating that "the patrons" had requested to see the ocean as they dined. Well, I knew what that meant. It didn't take a mathematician to figure out who they were talking about—unless they were respectfully referring to *Jack Frost* booking a reservation that evening. These yahoos were kowtowing to Vince Vaughn at the expense of *my* health and well-being (can you say, No tip, cowboy?).

And for the sake of shits and giggles (and since I'm on a roll), let me touch on the state of the food at this pop stand. When our food finally did arrive (and I got the circulation flowing in my extremities enough to gnaw at it), it looked good enough to eat. The presentation was great. Like all fine dining establishments, the food came on a huge white plate, the meal situated squarely in the middle with some kind of unexplainable sauce dripping over the side of the "food tower," creating exclusive "food art," crowned with the requisite sprig of something green and leafy: mint, perhaps. I gave the presentation a "10." Joan, my sister, ordered the lobster. It was a bit pricey, but she's never one to fuss about cost. She loves good food and is not afraid to pay for it (and besides, if it was good enough for V.V., then it was good enough for her, right?).

Like clockwork, our entrées arrived in all their glory (there was plenty of room next to our empty water glasses, mind you). We were starving; probably because we'd been sitting there (freezing) and watching those at the next table devour a whole meal, while we waited patiently for the bread basket that never came and the cocktails that were never refilled. (Actually, our food might not have looked all that good, now that I think about it. Ravenous as we were, we'd have eaten the ass end out of a hog at that point. They could have served us a freakin' hot dog and called it filet mignon and we wouldn't have batted an eye.) But from what I can remember, all of our food looked pretty darn appetizing—all except for Joan's. Something about her lobster looked a little strange.

It resembled something more of the jumbo prawn variety than lobster, more of a *bite* of lobster perhaps, than a whole tail or a succulent fillet. Let me put it this way: this "slipper lobster" was definitely not measured by the ounce; this baby was diced up by the gram for a cool fifty bucks. Typically, when the four of us go out to eat, we like to share our meals, sampling bites from each other's plates. But on this night, poor Joan couldn't afford to reciprocate; she might not have had enough energy for the hike back to the room (which was okay with us because we quite preferred Australian lobster, anyway). Luckily for her, the potato patty at the base of her food tower was packed with carbohydrates for a quick energy boost (enough to tide her over until breakfast, at least).

After we were done with the meal (and I use that term loosely), it was time for the bill. Ironically, the waiter didn't waste any time delivering that little gem tableside. We had already overheard the whole conversation about how the powers that be at the bistro had graciously comp'd Vinny's meal (not due to lack of service, that's for sure), so it only stood to reason that the establishment needed to make up that lost revenue somewhere, right? (Duh.) Well, might as well get it from the four yahoos from Podunk, cruising around in the Grand Marquis (who likely won their little overnighter on a game show, or something).

To date, that was possibly the most expensive meal I've ever consumed. Considering we didn't have any appetizers and only one round of cocktails and the bill came to almost four hundred dollars, it definitely ranks in the top three, at least!

One thing is for certain, when we checked out of the Bacara Hotel and Spa the next day, our bank account was depleted by seventeen hundred dollars, and we felt good about it. The accommodations were amazing. If you ever get the chance to go, I highly recommend it.

So yes, our intrepid foursome stepped proudly into the Grand Marquis and drove off the property. We had a story to tell: I had finally had a run-in with a celeb on our trip to California. Shit, we'd practically eaten dinner with Vince Vaughn! Well, we had, in effect, *bought him dinner*. Much like the Conrad Bain story, I think I will go with this version and make it my own; it just *sounds* better than "we got screwed at some swanky bistro in So-Cal, while all the servers played favorites to Mr. Hollywood Pants," don't you think?

13

It's My Butt; I Will Squeeze It into Tight Jeans If I Want To

Have you ever had one of those ideas that you wish you'd never had? One of those ideas that sounded good at the time, made perfect sense in your head, but when you actually went into action, you found out quickly that this was not going to be one of your best life experiences? I've read about people with brainstorms like these. You know, like the guy who lost his change in the pop machine, so he decided it would be a good idea to "shake it out" of the pop machine. That's right; he shook the machine, which landed on top of him, killing him instantly. Not a good plan. Or what about the guy who attempts to fire his shotgun, but when he pulls the trigger nothing happens? So, the obvious thing to do would be to turn the gun toward his face and fire it again, right? Yes it's true: these things *do* happen.

Now you're probably thinking that my "good idea" must have been a really bad one. (Well, not that bad if I've lived to tell about it, right?) To me, it was almost that bad! I have determined that I don't make my most appropriate and rational choices when I've been looking into a mirror while naked, or if I've just been to a self-help seminar, heard a sappy inspirational song, or looked at pictures from my high school yearbook (a.k.a. "skinny pics"). And on this particular day I'd loaded up the triple threat! I'd been looking in the mirror while naked, *and* I had just returned from a self-help seminar, where they played sappy inspirational songs for us. I didn't have a prayer. I should've just gotten into bed, pulled the covers over my head and waited it out, waited for the inspiration to pass (but that would not have made a very interesting chapter, now would it?).

So now that you know my mental state, it should not surprise you that I (once again) had found the answer to all my woes. I knew (finally) how to dig down deep within myself, take control of my life (again), and shed those unwanted pounds, once and for all (I'm good enough, I'm smart enough, and doggone it, people like me).

My great idea? I found the tightest pair of jeans that I had in my closet (that I could still button, that is) and—inch by painful inch—eased into them. I was going to wear them everyday until they no longer felt tight. That is it; that was the plan. I thought that I'd be so uncomfortable and so grossed out that I'd avoid all carbs as I would the bubonic plague. I wouldn't so much as eyeball an Oreo because I would be so eagerly aspiring to the day when these pants would barely stay up on my widdeling hips!

Now, when I say "tight," I mean tight! These babies were like a second skin. When I zipped them, I could hear those denim fibers scream for mercy. I could not have slipped so much as a microchip in the pockets, let alone my hands. When I walked, my legs didn't experience a full range of motion, and my love handles were muffin-topping proudly over the waistband. If that wasn't bad enough, I had to pair these Slacks of Death with a long, baggy shirt (so as not to totally embarrass myself). I don't own many shirts like these, so finding a cute one was another feat, in and of itself.

Heigh-ho, heigh-ho, it's off to church we go—on Day 1 of the *Tight Jeans Diet*. Except that before I could even leave the house I paused, struck by a certain sensation: I had to go to the bathroom. I only mention this because I'd been a little bit constipated for a few days, so feeling the urge to go was a welcome blessing (or so I thought). This also speaks to the fact that no one has yet invented the word that describes how tight these jeans were. They actually squeezed my intestines enough that I had to take a crap (I don't care who you are, that is freaking tight). They were "crap-tight" (look it up). So, part of me thought, *This is great!* Not only was I going to steer clear of the ice cream and cake, but I was also going to literally *shed* unwanted pounds. *Perfect!* Off to the bathroom I went. Since I was closer to the powder room, I chose to land there; it was too painful to maneuver up the stairs that lead to the master bathroom, where I would typically lay an egg.

What I hadn't considered, however, was the re-zipping process. I mean, I'd gotten the fly closed once, but apparently I had expanded since then, because the second time was not as easy. It physically hurt to zip up my "crap-pants" again (this was going to be a long week).

When I finally got back from church that day, my stomach hurt, my ass hurt, and my legs were begging for relief. I also had a major craving for chocolate chip mint ice cream. All I wanted to do was take off those damn pants, get into my roomy, comfy, non-confining sweat pants, and scoop up some icy heaven (cue the sappy inspirational song and those newly coined positive affirmations). I needed to talk myself out of the ice cream, fast. So, I decided right then and there, on Day 1 of *The Tight Jeans Diet*, that I could not eat *anything* unless I was wearing the jeans. So that meant I had a choice: I could stay in the jeans and indulge with the ice cream; or I could forgo the dessert, restore the circulation in my legs, and put on my sweats (hmm, what to do, what to do).

Now let's reflect for just a moment. Doesn't it seem a little pathetic in its own way that I'm even having this conversation with myself? I mean, how many people that you know would actually contemplate either choice? I was literally going to stay in the hell pants long enough to stuff my face with ice cream and then run to the bedroom and relieve myself by changing into my sweatpants. All of this, mind you, was in an effort to lose weight. So, how does eating ice cream fit into the equation in the first place? See how sick and twisted this whole issue is for me?

Well, at the end of Day 1, Sarah won. I took off the jeans (damn, my stomach hurt) and didn't eat the ice cream. So, all points considered, Day 1 was a success. One thing that I did not think through very well, however, was that this perverse diet caper had commenced on a Sunday—the Sunday before Thanksgiving.

By the morning of Day 2, I had already cheated. I made the executive decision to eat breakfast before pouring myself into the damn jeans. Relax; it's not as though I hogged down a doughnut, or anything (I didn't have any available). No. I nibbled a (small) serving of Smart Start cereal. Seriously, does that even count as breakfast?   Wearing the jeans to work that day made me feel like I owed everyone an explanation. I didn't want people around me to think I was oblivious to the fact that with each step my pants were literally shaving my legs for me. So I spent most of Day 2 apologizing to co-workers and avoiding the rest of society. It was what I like to call "a drive-thru day." (Why do you automatically assume I mean a drive-thru like *McDonald's*? I'm on a diet, remember?) I went to the drive-thru pharmacy, drive-thru photo, and drive-thru dry cleaners.

Now, technically, since I'm the diet guru who invented *The Tight Jeans Diet*, it is safe to say that I get to make up the rules as I go along. I get to play, pass, or counter offer with myself as these harebrained ideas surface. So, it being the week of Thanksgiving, I decided to take a break from the diet (you know: one, two, skip a few)—not because I was quitting (I am not a quitter), but because I couldn't find a way to wear those damn pants on an airplane. You know that when you travel, you pick your most comfortable pants to wear. There is limited leg room anyway, and *never* is there a more important time for you to be able to bend your freaking knees. Plus, how good would it be for my psyche to have hundreds of people standing in line behind me at the airport staring at my ass and asking themselves why such a normal looking woman would feel good about leaving the house in denim Saran Wrap pants? It's not like everyone would automatically assume, "Oh, she is on *The Tight Jeans Diet*—good for her." So, I made a conscious decision to go on my Thanksgiving trip, sans the pants (it was only for a few days).

While on my trip I enjoyed myself in comfortable, loose fitting cargo-style trousers. What's even better is the fact that these baggy pants were a size S (which you petite gals know stands for "small"). Truth be told, that is the only reason why I bought them in the first place. Anything that I can get in a size S (does it come in any other colors?) I am going to purchase (who cares if they are butt ugly?), simply because they are SMALL. Anyway, I was really glad about the decision to take a break from the tight pants for the trip. There is nothing worse that sitting on a plane for a few hours and not being able to circulate blood to your lower appendages.

I *will* have you know, in case you are wondering, that I put the jeans on again, once I returned home. They weren't any tighter (bonus), but that's not saying much. I don't think I would have noticed whether they were or not, but I'm voting for "were not." I wore them around for exactly one day. That's how long I lasted. Like all my past diet plans, my latest madcap scheme lasted less than one week. I guess I got tired of constantly tugging at my thighs to pull them out of my, um, how shall I say it . . . crotch.

As for the impulse to challenge myself? I got over it. I think I really learned my lesson this time, too. I mean, I think it's time to admit that I cannot outsmart my fat. I think my fat cells have determined that they are bought and paid for and they are not going anywhere. They are lurking just beneath my skin even now, mocking me. Laughing amongst themselves at the fact that they have, once again, won our battle of wills. They just wait me out. They all gather round (not like they have to travel to and fro; they are pretty much elbow to elbow down there) and place their little fat-cell bets with their pretend fat-cell currency, wagering how many days (or hours) the old bag will last this time.

Well, I have news for you fat cells. Just wait. I'm on the verge of a breakthrough here. I can feel it (again). I'm going to hatch the perfect diet idea to quash all other diet ideas (seriously this time). And when I do, watch out (literally, because it will likely involve a needle and a giant fat-sucking vacuum). All you fat cells are going down (never to be heard from again). Oh yes, be afraid; be very afraid my little spongy friends!

Okay, now I'm just being pathetic. I am having a conversation with my fat cells and threatening their very existence. I don't really have anything to back up these threats (yet), so I'll stop here and be the bigger person (no pun intended). For now, I will think of something productive and positive. (Speaking of which, I'd better dig up some of those positive affirmations that I worked so hard to pencil onto that three-by-five card.) I think it's time that I finally step out of the tight jeans and find other means to step into my brilliance. Hmm. I reckon I will list those denim pants on eBay tomorrow. Perhaps I can earn enough cash to invest in that new cellulite cream. (Hey, I might be on to something . . .)

14

Eating with Judy

I am proud to say that I have cultivated some great friendships in my lifetime. Some of us have been friends for many years, and I look forward to spending time with these people weekly. Because we are girls, we like to do girlie stuff: reading *In Touch*, going to movies, and gossiping over cocktails after work. I like these activities because I can do them with almost any of my friends and not need to spend the next week in therapy (because I feel like a failure after shopping with my rich friends, or feel like a loser-mom after talking about my parental shortcomings with my stay-at-home mom friends, or feel like an idiot after discussing politics with my smart friends). I label these girlie pastimes *Neutral Activities*. I can afford to participate in any of them and in all likelihood come out unscathed. There is

Sarah Nilsen

one normal daily activity that most women do together, however, which I wouldn't classify as "neutral." Can you guess what it is?

Let me start by asking a rhetorical question. Everyone eats, right? I mean, when it gets right down to it, we as human beings need food to survive. My mother always used to say "Your body is like a car: it needs fuel." (Funny, she hasn't had to say that to me in about ten years. Probably safe to say that I got the point, Mom). The answer to the question is: NO, not *everyone* eats, and I've just recently come to terms with this phenomenon. So why is it that some women just don't eat? (I guess there could be a man out there that does not eat as well, but I have yet to meet, one face to face. I imagine he's out there *not eating* with the Abominable Snowman right about now). I mean, these non-eaters obviously eat something to stay alive, but they don't eat for recreation: they only eat when they're hungry. Strange. I bet they don't even think about food unless they are eating it. And, unless someone hands them a menu, it's doubtful they even contemplate their next caloric windfall.

This must be some kind of genetic defect, or something—like a missing chromosome that prevents them from appreciating the calming effects of chocolate, perhaps. Whatever the case, these women make me nervous. I don't know if it is because I think that at any time they might swoop down and abduct me for some fat-related experiment on their mother ship, or if it is just the fact that when I'm around adult women who don't eat, I am suddenly overwhelmed with anxiety. What if they expect me to join them in their voluntary (for no good reason) fasting?

Enter my good friend, Judy. Judy and I see each other often. She is about twenty-five pounds lighter than I am (you see where this is going), but I have chosen to overlook that little fact because she is a lifelong friend and I forgive her for being thinner than me. (I am, however, way smarter than she is. Did I mention that smart is the new skinny?) In any case, I agreed to go to lunch with her last week. It must have been in a moment of weakness, however, because I know better than that. I other stick to other "neutral" activities with Judy. In a nutshell, it was all one big therapy session waiting to happen.

As we we're looking over the menus and chatting about kids and work, I found myself getting nervous about placing my order. That pepperoni pizza looked really good. In fact, it was known to be the best pizza in the city. Oh boy! I was salivating at the thought of it when Judy spoke.

"I'm starving!" she declared.

Had she just said what I thought she'd said? *She* was hungry? Yahoo! That meant that we would actually *eat* this time. (Sometimes I feel like we don't really "lunch" anymore. It's more like we go to a restaurant and bitch about our lives over iced tea, sans the sweetener, of course, and a few sprigs of mint.) Last I checked, lunch was supposed to be a meal—one of three meals for the day, as a matter of fact—and a few pieces of lettuce and cold tea leaves do not make a meal. So when she announced that she was hungry, I knew this was my lucky day, I knew we were going to order something of substance and real sustenance this time.

That pepperoni pizza would hit the spot! Should we share one, or should we each get our own so that we could take some home and have cold pizza again for breakfast? Did I have the guts to ask if she would dare eat pizza twice in a row? Should I just keep quiet, let her take the lead and order first? I had to think fast; the waitress was approaching.

"I'll have the pepperoni pizza," I blurted out (so much for riding shotgun). I glanced at Judy for approval.

No sooner had I gotten the words out than Judy ordered: a small side salad, no croutons, no dressing, and lemon water.

"I haven't eaten a thing all day!" she explained.

WHAT? Had she just changed the rules on me, mid-date? I thought she was hungry. I thought she was going to consume human food this time. She hadn't eaten all day and this was what she chose to silence her hunger pangs?

Well, guess what Judy, I thought to myself. *I have eaten today.* As a matter of fact, I'd started my day off with a chocolate bar I confiscated from my son (after all, he shouldn't eat so much candy before breakfast), then I had yogurt (well, frozen yogurt in my smoothie, but that counts as yogurt), and then I polished off a bag of Famous Amos cookies that had been left on my desk from the day before. All that being said, I was still going to eat lunch as normal people would at this time of day. Pizza!

By the way, why was she telling me she was "so hungry" and then ordering a salad without any meat or croutons or any flavor, whatsoever? (Was this the point where I should recognize that it was no coincidence that I had twenty-five pounds on her? 'Cause if so, I'd like to strike that thought from the record and remain in denial, thank you). Why couldn't she just keep those comments to herself? I could see that she hadn't eaten all day, and from the looks of it, she did not exactly gorge yesterday, either.

The waitress returned with our drinks and a bread basket. Oh, sweet Jesus! That bread was still warm from the oven: steaming, beckoning, luring me toward the dark side. Was it polite for me to indulge? God knows, she wasn't going to eat it. But I quickly remembered Rule #1 in the girlfriend handbook: "Thou shall not carb-load."

Apparently, going for the bread basket at a meal with the girls held the social equivalent of whipping out a mirror and cutting up a line of cocaine right there at the restaurant. Instead we were supposed to view those carbs in disgust, as if our waiter had just dropped a basket of manure on the dining table and we were simply waiting for someone to whisk it away.

Meanwhile, Judy was not exactly helping me out here.

Okay, I thought to myself, *so then, we're expected to play the Ignore the Bread Basket Game.* For those unfamiliar with the rules, let me explain to you how this game works. Everyone pretends they don't see the bread in the center of the table. We all go on talking about life, the gym membership we just got, or the new naturopath that we're seeing. (Of course, during this game I can barely keep up with the conversation because all I'm thinking about is the damn bread.) There's some kind of female code that says the game is over when one person breaks under pressure and makes the first move, reaching toward the basket for that first fragrant piece. Then it's every woman for herself. All of a sudden, that piping hot basket of manure has a little more appeal. Then all the girls at the table follow suit: it is now acceptable to eat the bread. But don't think that this game has a happy ending. Quite the contrary: the poor girl who buckled under has been blacklisted as the "carb-whore." As a rule, she must not be the first to reach for the dinner rolls again for at least a year. (She probably cannot even be seen within ten feet of a carbohydrate for at least a few weeks, and she better have her ass on a treadmill in the meantime). End of game. (Seems rational, right?)

Glancing again at Judy, I got the feeling that it was time for the Ignore the Bread Game, but I was also picking up the vibe that she truly had no interest in the bread basket anyway (is this possible?). She wasn't even eyeballing it. She did not appear to be contemplating whether or not she should just take a piece. Truth be told, I was willing to give her a "freebie-carb." She hadn't eaten all day, and I knew what that felt like (well, not really, but I could imagine it, and it sucked). I didn't want her to suffer any longer.

Call me carb-obsessed, but while Judy was talking about something to do with the copy machine, her new imported silk blouse, and the ink cartridge, all I heard was "Blah, blah, blah . . . *bread.*"

I knew full well that I wouldn't be having any because I'd been the first to take a piece at a girls' dinner last July (which, by my count, was only four months ago); therefore I couldn't take a piece today. (If Judy hadn't been there to see me take that piece at the girls' dinner, did that count? I determined it was too risky to chance it.) I silently declined the bread and did my best to pay attention to whatever it was she was yakking about (assuming it was all about her anyway, but that is another chapter).

When the pizza arrived, I was not even hungry. It's no fun to *eat* with someone who doesn't *eat*. I would feel that with every bite of my greasy meal she would be looking at me with a silent question: "are you seriously going to put that into your body?" It would be like going shopping with someone who doesn't buy anything. Once you realize that you are the only one doing the shopping, it's no longer a team sport. It sort of takes the thrill of being bad out of it.

Though my pizza looked good, with Judy the human signpost sitting next to me munching salad, I felt like some kind of Glutton Bowl contestant. I had lost my appetite. I realized that I liked eating with my fat friends because not only do they eat with me, but they worry about me if I do *not* eat. I mean, they aren't *really* fat. They're *normal.* But to someone like Judy, who would consider any waist measurement over 26-inches obese, they are fat.

I pecked and poked at my pizza while Judy nattered on and on about how she needed to get her size 2 pants altered (can they even alter a size 2?) before some big party on the weekend. At this point, I needed her to shut up. I needed her to cram some of that tasteless salad on her little fork and stick it in her pie hole! (Do thin people even have a "pie" hole? Do thin people even get this analogy?) Things got even better when she went on to talk about how bloated she was, because it was "her time of the month" (anyone got any duct tape?). I am sorry, but if she *indulges* in lettuce during her "time of the month," I'm really doomed to a life of blubber. Who craves salad? God! Could she just stop now?

Judy laid her fork down with a heavy sigh, as if her little body couldn't take one more bite, lest it detonate. She was done with her lunch. Completely satisfied. She probably would not even *think* about food again until the next morning. (I, on the other hand, had spent the last fifteen minutes contriving a plan to swing by McDonald's after our lunch so I could eat in peace).

Life is so unfair. I don't even know why I agreed to eat with her that day. I'm not even sure why I continue to be her friend. She evidently has no concept of my mom's idea: that the body is like a car. I hope she gets gas!

15

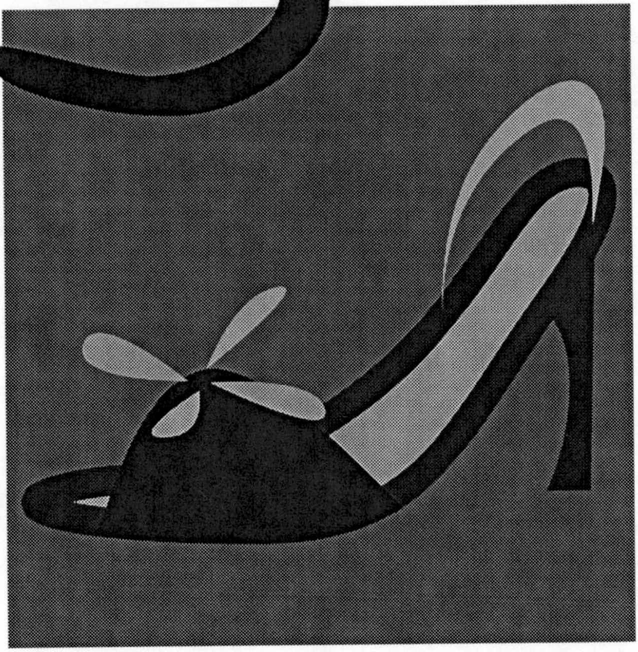

Ellen DeGenerous?

There are several milestones in one's life, and I've been blessed to reach some of them already. Turning thirty was one of those milestones that I was determined to make memorable (come hell or high water). So, instead of silently waiting for my husband to plan something for me and risk being disappointed, I decided to plan my own birthday events. (And for the record, my husband did pull through for me and threw me a great surprise party the week after my birthday. He's the greatest!)

On my birthday, which is in February, I recruited my sister Jeni and my mom to take me on a trip to California. We had two things on the docket for our trip. First, we needed to visit the trendy clothing store, Kitson, which I always read about in my gossip magazines (I knew that if I got into that store I was bound to see someone famous and then my life would be somehow complete). The other thing that I wanted to do was see *The Ellen DeGeneres Show*, which is taped in Burbank. So, I booked the trip, got tickets for a taping of the show, and we were all set to head down to the Golden State to ring in my "adulthood" in style on Rodeo Drive.

Like all my harebrained ideas that had preceded this one, a few weeks before the trip I was up late one night, thinking about what would make the event even more perfect. (Light bulb moment!) I had the (brilliant) idea that I'd bring all my spa products to *The Ellen DeGeneres Show* and offer to give her entire staff a foot-soak before (or after) the taping. It would be such a nice gesture that she couldn't help but love me, and she'd probably give me a great photo-op as well as an even greater story to tell all my friends back home—about how I wasn't afraid to step outside my comfort zone (you know, ask and you shall receive) and create my own destiny. Perfect.

So, first I needed to figure out how to reach the appropriate person on her staff that would be able to hook up this kind of event for me. This took a little research (plus a little embellishing of who I was and what I did) *and* a little time, but I finally landed the name and address of a production manager. Next, I wrote a letter to this guy, telling him that I was "going to be in the area" and would be happy "to extend my services" to the staff as a "courtesy." I made it all sound very professional and very fun. I thought for sure that Ellen, of all people, would be jumping at the opportunity to get some down time with the gals and relax after a hard day of interviews and dancing (I am sure her dogs were barkin'). Along with the letter, I also sent some of our best-selling body butter in the mango scent. No one can resist this stuff, so I thought it would soon be a done deal.

By the time I got the package in the mail to *The Ellen Show*, I only had a few days until I had to leave for the trip, so I needed to know if I was going to be able to pull this off or not. If I didn't need to bring all my supplies for a foot soak, then that made a bit of an impact on the way I packed my suitcase, if you get my drift. Well, the days came and went and I never heard back from the show. I left a few messages with the production manager, but he never returned my calls. But I didn't feel defeated; I still had a chance to ask Ellen in person when I got to the sound stage for the taping. Perhaps I could wow her with my charm and then she would invite me back to do the event with her staff at a later time, right? And, if all else failed, there was still Rodeo Drive waiting for me (and that is nothing to scoff at).

On the day of the taping—my thirtieth birthday—Jeni, my mom and I were all very excited to see *The Ellen Show*. We'd never been to a live taping of anything before, so this might as well have been the Super Bowl. The taping was scheduled for two o'clock in the afternoon, so we planned to spend the morning hanging out around Burbank and checking things out. As we passed by the studio where the show was recorded, we noticed a line forming—and it was only nine o'clock in the morning. We thought this was really strange, considering that we had tickets for the show. It wasn't like we were vying for a spot, so it didn't make much sense to us that people would be lined up so far in advance (these people must be from Minnesota, or something). They were all set up with lawn chairs, umbrellas, and sack lunches. (Did the forecast call for rain? It was California, for crying out loud.) I swear I even saw a *Hibachi*.

Without paying too much attention to the pathetic tourists, we pressed on and toddled around the area, hoping to catch a glimpse of a few actors from *Days of Our Lives* (which is shot at a nearby sound stage).

About two hours before taping began, we noticed that the line was really long, so we decided to go ahead and join the crowd. I should tell you that since I was, in essence, making my television debut, I was decked out in a great outfit complete with some really hot (and really expensive and totally impractical) shoes. I had on some cute Capri pants and a thin sweater set. Yes, I know it was the middle of February (I already heard the speech from my mom, thank you), but this was, after all, California. Coming from Seattle, any place dry was sufficient cause to break out the sundress, if you know what I mean, because you were on vacation.

Did I say dry? Well, I must have spoken too soon, because about the time we claimed our place in line, it began to rain. Notice I didn't say, "I noted a light sprinkle in the warm California air." No sir, this was a full-out downpour, right in the middle of Universal Studios that fateful afternoon, two full hours before my two hundred dollar blow-out would finally find cover, and two hours and fifteen minutes before my ass would be on national television—looking more like a drowned rat than a buxom thirty-year-old on her way to Rodeo Drive.

There I was in all my glory, standing on the sidewalk with a few hundred other hopefuls—with nowhere to go to get out of the rain. With each passing minute my hair got frizzier, my clothes got wetter, and my toes got colder. I would've given my eyeteeth for a coat (but I didn't tell my mom that; I was not going to give her the satisfaction). The only thing that kept me in that line was knowing that in a few hours I was going to be face to face with one of my favorite comedians: Ellen DeGeneres. So what if I was drenched, right? Maybe she'd feel sorry for me and offer up her dressing room for me to primp, or something (hey, stranger things have happened).

We were about an hour into this love-fest when one of her staffers came out to the line and started handing out some kind of tickets. He started at the front of the line and then worked his way toward the back, handing each person a piece of paper with a number on it. I thought this was odd because as far as I knew, we already had tickets (well, at least *we* did, and that was all that mattered). He had one hundred fifty-seven tickets to hand out. How do I know this? Because I was number one hundred fifty-eight. You got it: we had just been axed out of the "super ticket" club. I could not wait to find out what goodies we were missing out on. I was sure it was not back stage passes; there were too many handed out. I knew it was not invitations to a special post-show party at Ellen's place; she couldn't bus that many (wet) fans to her house. Maybe these people were flagged for the security search, or something, and they would be held up emptying all their bags and belongings at the gate while we (the ones who did not waste our day standing in line like idiots) sauntered past the guards, then filed into our (primo) seats in the warm studio and mingled with Ellen, helping her pick out the day's playlist with the DJ.

Actually, to my surprise the nice gentleman was not handing out security tickets. He was, in fact, handing out legitimate tickets to the show. (But Sarah, you had tickets already, right? you ask.) Well, I thought I did. But apparently there are people who obtain tickets to these types of events and then fail to show up at the taping. So to avoid having too many empty seats (which does not look good on TV), the studio gives out more tickets than there are seats. Only problem is, no one told me this before I booked a ticket to fly out of state, persuaded my sister to take time off work, begged my mom to come with us, left my family, built my birthday dreams around meeting Ellen DeGeneres, spent half of my birthday standing on the sidewalk in the pouring-down rain, ruining my shoes and freezing my tits off for one reason: parking my thirty-year-old ass in the studio so I could dance with Ellen! Now, I had some yahoo telling me that my ticket didn't count? That I was going home empty-handed? No stories of meeting Ellen? No invite to do my foot soak with the crew? No souvenirs except the puddle of California rain water that had accumulated in my outlandishly over-priced shoe?

The nice staffer informed us that we needed to continue to "wait and see." He explained that once those one hundred fifty-seven seats were filled, it all came down to the matter of how many VIPs showed up for the taping (was he taunting me?). Basically, the more important people that showed up (whom we might never get the chance to see), the less room they'd have for peons like us. But then he unloaded the "good news." (Good because I had been waiting for the silver lining. After all it was my damn birthday.) He explained that we could wait in the Riff Raff Room and watch the taping from backstage. Hello-o-o-h, you might as well watch it at home. At least if you're at home you don't have to wait in line for the bathroom, you're not getting eyeballed by the gal next to you who looks like a human Barbie doll (she must hail from Laguna Beach), and you can go to the fridge for some ice cream (for comfort, of course) when you need it.

Another hour went by. We were still standing in the rain. Only now it was worse, because now we were not only cold and wet; we were pissed, too. We were wet, pissed-off women. The only thing worse than a pissed-off woman who is cold and wet is a woman that keeps reminding you *"it's my birthday"* every three minutes (like that somehow trumps the fact that everyone else behind her in line, who is also not getting a seat in the studio, is also cold, wet and pissed off).

Finally the line started moving (thank you, God). By this time we were not even attempting to cover our heads with our forearms or huddle together. Nope, our blood was boiling enough to keep us plenty warm. Slowly, but surely, we made our way into the studio like cattle heading to feed. As we entered the shelter of the studio, those do-gooders who had umbrellas (the show-offs) shook off their parcels—while we wrung out our sweaters. They ran their fingers through their (dry) hair—while we blew on our hands in a desperate attempt to restore feeling in our fingertips. If you were a fly on the wall, you could've done a quick scan of the room and definitely discerned who had watched the forecast and who had not.

We waited in the Riff Raff Room for several minutes. A few staffers came in and out and gave some simple instructions to the people who had tickets, or should I say, *legit* tickets (whatever). The rest of us just sort of sat there contemplating the other things we could have been doing with our day. I didn't know about the rest of the group, but I had no shortage of ideas because after all . . . *it was my stinkin' birthday!*

When the time came to file into the studio to begin the taping, all the excited ticket holders stood erect, waiting for their numbers to be called. Some of them eyed us with pity as they entered the studio (did I mention it was my birthday?). Others, however, were careful not to make eye contact with the low-life wannabes littering their air space. My mom and Jeni and I just sat with our backs to the wall and hoped that our lucky number would get called, and we desperately wished that one of the VIPs would miss a plane so we could get into the studio for the taping.

Then we heard it. The words rolled over us in slow motion, but we were able to make them out.

"Number one hundred fifty-eight through one hundred—" (Who the hell cared; we were in and that was all that mattered.)

We jumped up from our seats and headed to the stairs to join the rest of our posse "on the other side." (Too bad for the rest of the wannabes: pathetic, really. It was kind of cute how they were all dressed up to see Ellen. They should've gotten in line a little earlier. Everyone knows that.)

The good news was that since it was the VIPs that didn't show up, we would be taking *their* seats. So, guess what that meant? You got it, baby. We were sitting smack in the front row! It was me, and then Ellen (well, me, then the big, annoying cameraman, and then Ellen, but who's counting?)! No sooner did we sit down than we had to get up and start dancing with our girl, Ellen. It was great.

Great, except for the fleeting moment when I realized that I'd likely be caught on camera in all my post-rainstorm glory. My amazing outfit had turned to mush. My expensive salon Style-and-Go looked more like a Style-Oh-No, and my poor shoes made their own noises when I walked because they were so waterlogged. This wasn't exactly the hip Thirty Debut I'd hoped for when I booked the tickets to California, but at this point I was content just to be *inside* the studio proper. The fact that I looked like a rescue swimmer was just par for the course, I guess.

Ellen didn't disappoint me. She was amazing, funny, and worth the wait. Even though she didn't single me out and ask me about my mind-blowing body butter (I'm not even sure it ever made it to her desk), I still hold out hope that someday, somehow, I'll meet her personally. If anyone from her staff is reading this, my offer still stands. I am happy to come down and give you all a fun afternoon with a relaxing foot soak after a hard day's work (God knows, you all deserve it after crushing the dreams of hopeful audience members all day). Next time, however, I think I'll offer my services in the summer; and you'll have to agree to pencil my mom, my sister, and myself on your VIP list.

My Annual Annual

Everyone does it. It's covered by insurance. It's the "right" thing to do, they say. But still, it feels a little more like "D-Day" to me.

I am talking about my annual exam at the gynecologist, of course. I know this is something that all women must endure, part of the curse of being the superior species, I suppose. But knowing this doesn't make my trip to the OB-GYN any less horrifying for me.

I should tell you that the thought of another woman having to examine my "who-who" is not the part that freaks me out. That whole experience, while a little unsightly, doesn't gross me out. The worst part comes *before* the actual exam.

I called to make the appointment about four weeks ago. I penciled it into my Franklin Covey so as not to forget (as if that's going to happen). I also made a lunch date with my girlfriend afterward (you know, the person who I can really *eat* with, guilt-free). Now begins the weekly analysis of my dietary issues. (I have three weeks to lose weight before I have to get on the scale at the doctor's office. Wow, where did that week go? Okay, now I have two weeks to get into shape: one week to starve myself, then two days on a liquid diet and I should be okay. You get the point.) I'll spare you the pathetic details of this whole ritual and skip right to the meat and potatoes (did someone say potatoes? YUM!) of this story.

Today is the day. I start the morning off with a thirty-minute appointment in my closet. What to wear? It has to be something lightweight (no brainer) and slightly cute (if I'm going to be fat, I had better be cute). I have determined that I must wear my hair down (even thought hair clips are plastic, they're not light). I have also chosen a skirt to wear (good call since this has to weigh less than a pair of pants, for sure) and boots (easy on, easy off). The outfit is quite cute, I must say. Since it's September, I should finish off this ensemble with a light jacket . . . wait, a vest (even better, a vest it is).

I walk into the office (looking cute) and proceed to check in at the counter. I'm eyeballing the competition—a few pregnant gals waiting in the lobby. (Don't you hate the way pregnant women look totally cute with that little basketball under their shirt? That's another chapter I guess, but remind me to rant about life's cruel joke later.) I also look to see if I recognize any of the nurses from my last visit.

That's when I notice her. Oh my God, say it isn't so! I totally know this nurse; she graduated from high school with me. She knew me back in my glory days when I was a size zero. I had one rocking body back then, a full head of (real) blonde hair, and a taut tummy to boot. This was before adult acne set in and my boobs went south—

along with my laugh lines. Nice! Perhaps most importantly, the last time I saw her I was a hundred pounds soaking wet; now I am, well . . . not. Shit! I quickly send a prayer up to the Big Guy and beg for her not to be my nurse. *Please do not let her call my name. Please, please do not let her take me to the Scale of Truth.*

Ironically, however, as I take a long look at her, I notice she looks really old. I mean, she looks like someone's mom (and not an M.I.L.T.F., mind you). She looks at least ten years older than I do. I hold my gaze on her long enough to see her come out from behind the counter, and . . . JACKPOT! She has packed on a few pounds herself over the years. Yeah, from the looks of it, she has not exactly been shying away from the buffet, either. Okay, so worst case scenario, if she has to do the deed with me, she can't really make any comments on *my* weight gain, because she can match me pound for pound, AND she looks like she could be my mom. So, game on. I am feeling pretty good.

Come to find out, this is a moot point; another nurse calls my name a few minutes later. She leads me to a chair to take my blood pressure (so far so good). Then she tells me to "hop on the scale."

Now, is it just me, or have some of these nurses lost their bedside manner? *Hop on the scale*, as if this is a joy to do? As if I have been looking forward to gleefully hopping on the scale so that she can record my weight in the "Chart of Truth (and Disgust)." Who *hops* on the scale, anyway? I think she should have said, "When you're ready, Sarah, take your place on the scale" or, "I'll leave the room and you can record your own weight. We're on the honor system at this clinic."

Well, it goes without saying that I cannot do any "hopping" until I've unloaded all the items that will skew the results. So I take off the boots, take off the vest (unload the lint from my pockets), and try not to look like a self-absorbed idiot as I lay it all down on the nearby desk. It feels like I'm going through a cavity search at the airport security checkpoint, or something: anything that is not attached comes off.

She is standing over me rolling her eyes (come on, as if I'm the only one who does this) with her red pen ready to record. (I wonder if she even has a soul.) I get on the scale (trust me, I do not hop) and await my fate. She fiddles with the metal things on the scale. For a minute I contemplate whether I should look or not. But I guess she has the last laugh because she announces my weight in a voice I swear everyone can hear in the back of the office (thanks, bitch). By the way, she freaking *rounded up*! I can see where it settled on the line, and she rounded *up*! Who rounds up? That should be rule *número uno*: You never round *up* when weighing a woman. Don't they teach that stuff in Nursing 101? It probably took me three days to lose that half a pound. I probably said no to a weeks'worth of desserts to drop that weight, and she has the audacity to round up (if there's a customer complaint card, I am *so* filling one out). She can take her little red pen and her fuzzy math and "hop" herself right out into traffic!

After the (fraudulent) weigh-in, I am escorted back to the examination room, where I'm asked to take my clothes off, then drape this tissue-thin "cover" over my lap and wait for the doctor (who will only be a "minute"). As I undress (and hide my oversized, sweat-stained bra neatly under my skirt, so as not to gross anyone out), I can literally feel my body temperature decrease (let me escort you to the Jack Frost Suite). The room has to be a balmy 55 degrees. I sit up on the table and drape the oversized tissue over my legs and wait. A few minutes go by; I have already chewed off all my nails and still, no doctor. A few more minutes drag by. I've learned all about STD's, IUD's and HIV (thanks to the handy pamphlets that line the nearby wall), and still, no doctor. Now I have to pee. What is the deal? I am cold, hungry, bored, *and* I have to pee. What could be worse? (Oh wait, a cold spatula heaved up my "who-who" by a German woman named Olga.)

Finally the doctor arrives. She's been my doctor for many years, so she likes to chat a bit before the exam. (You know, exchange pleasantries before she invades my privates with the metal prod.) She asks me how I'm doing, do I have any concerns, how the kids are. Then we get down to business.

"Scooch to the end of the table, Sarah," she says. (What the hell is a scooch, anyway?)

I ease myself down the length of the table and put my feet in the stirrups. (I am instantly reminded of childbirth. Suddenly, cold, hungry and bored doesn't seem so bad.)

"Relax your knees," she suggests.

(Okay, relax, I forgot. Let's see, lady, I'm cold, hungry, and I have to pee. You're about to stick a foreign object inside of me and scrape for unidentified growth, and you do it all with a smile. It's kind of freaking me out, to tell you the truth; relaxing is not an option here, okay?)

"So," she says, "I took my daughter to the Hilary Duff concert last night."

Is she kidding me? We're going to talk about her adventures with a Pop Princess while I am naked, cold, and hungry, doing my darnedest not to unload that iced tea I drank this morning all over her? The time for small talk has passed, Doc; we need to get in and get out, if you know what I mean. (And why is she thinking about a concert while she is examining me, anyway? I mean, I guess there are worse things for her to think about. At least she didn't say, "So, I had some really bad cauliflower last night," or something.)

A swab here, a push there, and it's all over. Whew! I'm done. I can cross this visit off the list of To-Dos and go about my life again. It wasn't so bad really; I mean, it could have been worse. I'm thankful that I didn't get weighed by my high school friend. I'm happy that no bells or other warnings of malfunction went off when I "hopped" on the scale. As far as I know, no one else has access to my chart (so I can cheerfully remain in denial about my real weight). The doctor didn't find anything out of the ordinary during my exam (always a good sign). Life is good.

Now it's time to keep that lunch appointment I made earlier with my best girlfriend. (After spending the last few weeks being paranoid about my weigh-in at the doctor, I need a release.) I love eating with her because she is not my *skinny* friend: she is my *best* friend, Kara. We'll gab about our weight, talk smack about mutual friends, complain about our husbands, and brag about our kids. I'm really looking forward to our lunch because I know that I can order anything off the menu without so much as a wince out of her, and she can as well!

When we finally sit down to eat, we both order a salad (I also order some quesadillas "to start"). I begin telling her about my experience at the OB-GYN. I'm sort of going on about the temperature in the doctors office, and mentioning the gal I knew from school (she knows her, too, so she feels my pain) and how she was working there. But the one thing that really stands out about our conversation is the comment she makes about those ridiculous paper gowns.

I've already explained to her how I had to use the bathroom during my visit, but how I couldn't because I didn't want to have to get dressed again and go use the restroom. She looks me dead in the eye and says, "Oh, I just go right in my gown."

So I look her dead in the eye right back and say, "No Kidding? Are those gowns really that absorbent?"

She just smiles sweetly and says, "I cannot believe you just asked me that."

At this moment I know we'll be friends forever. Not because she's the first person to split a piece of pie with me, or allow me a trip to the bread basket without question, but because I'd never want her to get pissed off at me and share our little conversation with anyone else.

17

My Pet Peeves

I have been waiting all my life for the opportunity to share my Top Ten Pet Peeves with someone who will listen. I figure this is my moment (you already paid for the book; you might as well read the chapter, right?). Here it goes.

1. Sitting in the back of an airplane

Can I just tell you?—I would almost rather have the plane go down mid-flight than discover that I'm seated in row 39 out of 39. I literally just about O.D. on anxiety when I have to fly one of those airlines that do not assign seats prior to boarding. It's like lotto, when you never know what you're going to get. It amazes me that I always seem to be the one in the armpit of the jetliner, regardless of when I booked my reservations.

For all you First Class Frequent Flyer snobs that have never visited the back of the aircraft, allow me to elaborate. In the back row there are a few things working against you. First of all, the seats do not recline. I don't know about you, but I'm the sneaky passenger that tries to get away with reclining before takeoff (even though you're clearly supposed to wait until you reach a comfortable cruising altitude). I recline just enough to take some of the tension out of my back, but not so much that the stewardess is likely to notice, unless she is really paying attention (an art I've perfected over several cross-country flights). If I see her looking my way, I make sure to be overly nice (hoping she'll let me off without making me bring my seat to its full upright position). I do the same thing at the end of the flight. When the captain tells us that we are "preparing for landing," and he requests that we return our seats to the most uncomfortable position, I pretend I'm sleeping and did not hear the announcement. That tactic usually buys me a few extra minutes of "comfort." (You can use that tip if you want to—a freebie for you.) Well, in the back of the bus the seats don't recline at all! There's nothing worse than this in my book. I know you might be thinking that we're talking about all of a 10-degree angle here (it's not like we're lounging in a La-Z-Boy or anything), but without it, I might as well be inverted.

Next, the seats in the back are ALWAYS next to the bathroom (the one in coach, reserved for the riff-raff). So, not only are you forced to sit erect for five hours, but if you dare to look toward the aisle, you will find someone else's ass in your face from the time you take off until the time you land. And I say "ass" not in a good way. It is not like "Oh, check it out. Nice jeans, dude!" No. This is not the kind of "sights" I am trying to illustrate. I'm talking about plumbers crack, bohemian B.O., dirty diaper, sweaty, stanky ass.

Three inches from your face. The. Whole. Trip. Couple that with the fact that your own butt goes to sleep from the obnoxious vibration of the jet engine, thrumming away directly under your seat (and that's the only part of you that can sleep because it is so damn loud back there), and the screaming hunger pangs you get because you're almost ready to land before the food cart ever works its way back to you (the food is always cold by the time you get finally get it), and you're probably beginning to see my point. I also feel the need to mention that by the time it's your turn for a beverage, they're down to a slim choice: *Ginger Ale* or *Fresca*.

Needless to say, I'm sure you can sense my passionate stance on the situation. Life in the last row is a fate I don't wish on anyone. As a matter of fact, I say that we use this as a method to extract information from spies. Put them on a transatlantic flight in the back (non-reclining) row, and even the most tight-lipped terrorist will sing like a canary. Try it. You'll see.

2. Grocery Shopping

Am I alone on this one? I hate grocery shopping. If you asked me which aspect of it I dislike, I would say all of it. I don't like filling my cart, I don't like spending too much money for boxed cereal, I don't like unloading the car, and I don't like cooking. I don't have a lot to say about it, other than it's something that I put off doing as long as possible. I will literally find a way to eat out every meal until my husband finally says that he can't stand it one more day and makes me go to the grocery store. I should say that, where I live, there are not a lot of places to eat out. We spend more time going out to eat at the local hospital (no joke), because they at least attempt to prepare meals that aren't going to compromise my perfect physique (are you on the floor rolling in laughter?). Seriously, at least at the hospital cafeteria I can feel like I made an effort to feed my family something healthy that doesn't come with a "toy" in the box. All of this in an effort to avoid the supermarket. That's all I can say on the subject. Let me know if you find a way to get food into my cupboards that does not involve me driving, buying, and loading; then let me know if you find a way to fry it up in a pan and serve it to my family without me having to mix it, cook it, or clean it, and I will nominate you for the Nobel Peace Prize. (For a complete list of all the other domestic duties that I choose to omit, please refer to the rest of this book.)

3. Mega-Movie Theaters

I love going to the movies. I go all the time; I even go alone (pathetic and sad, I know). But I've recently been introduced to the new "mega theaters" that have sprouted up around the country. These are, like, 25-Plexes that show *all* the movies *all* the time. I went to one last weekend in Arizona. They had all the new movies playing on multiple screens. (I think they even had "Raiders of the Lost Ark" still playing.) I stood patiently in line for about fifteen minutes while ONE employee sold tickets. That wasn't the part that really got me. It was the snack counter. This movie theater had too many choices. I literally waited for twenty minutes for one couple in front of me to place their order. Their order came to almost one hundred U.S. dollars! They had hot food choices (appetizers, I guess) and cold food choices, drinks and snacks. As a matter of fact, I'm not even sure if they were there to see a movie, or if they were just there for dinner (she must not like to grocery shop either). I couldn't believe the mecca of salty sensations and sweet treats that were on display. This theater didn't have just one snack bar; they had five different counters to purchase food. The walk to the theater that was showing our movie took me about six minutes. I missed half the previews just navigating my way around the megaplex. I had to stop to pee twice before I found the door marked "Theater 19."

The reason this is so disturbing to me is that I feel the cinema has gotten out of hand. I like to see a flick as much as the next guy (gal), but I don't want to have to arrive two hours early to make sure I'm in my seat before the show starts. They are already charging an arm and a leg for tickets these days; now I have to go "90 days, same-as-cash financing" just so I can enjoy some popcorn and a soda, too. (Did you think I was one of those losers who sneak in treats because I'm too cheap to fork out $23.00 for a small popcorn?) The next thing we know, we'll be able to see a movie, drop off our dry cleaning, see our gynecologist, and buy a fishing license—all at the megaplex (welcome to the AMC Teriyaki, Bait and Tackle Megaplex). Let's keep things simple shall we? Charge me a decent price to see the movie, spoil me with popcorn and nachos with "cheez" from a pump, and leave me enough cash in my wallet so that I can afford the gas to get home, will ya?

4. Pregnant girls, the ones you can't tell are pregnant from behind

They have a little belly going on in the front, yet claim complete "sex kitten status" from the back. Not. Fair. (Didn't your mother ever teach you the value of being a *well-rounded* person? What, pray tell, did you think she was talking about? Duh!) Enough said.

5. When the drive-thru person messes up my "special order"

I won't mention any names (Tacos 2 Go), but there is only one drive-thru fast food chain where I can eat without a total relapse of guilt. I only like one item from their entire menu. I order it made one specific way. It is not hard. It is not rocket science to prepare my meal to my particular fancy, yet for some reason, I'd say that they get it right about twenty-five percent of the time.

I order the chicken soft taco—*light*—in a meal: no cheese, no sour cream, and extra salsa. How hard is that?

Every time I order it, the worker always corrects me and says, "We don't serve sour cream on the chicken soft taco *light,* only salsa." To which I always reply, "Okay, just salsa then, and no cheese." (And what do I get when I *don't* specify "no sour cream?" Gobs of it.)

When I first started ordering my taco, I used to literally crave it. Seriously, there isn't even a Tacos 2 Go near my office. I can either drive all the way across town to get one (or shall I say, send my assistant, Staci, to do it), or I can go to the mall, park the car, then walk into the food court and order one to go. Neither is a very convenient choice, but because I love this damn taco so much, I make the sacrifice (or Staci does). The meal never disappoints me. It always hits the spot. Until recently, that is. I don't know if the eatery has undergone some new management or what, but I swear to God, I cannot get the taco the way I like it to save my life. It's to the point now where I don't even want to see it. I gingerly open the tortilla as if a snake might pop out, or something (already knowing it's not going to be "right").

I either wind up with *extra* cheese (instead of no cheese), *low fat* sour cream (instead of no sour cream), or *no* salsa (instead of extra salsa). And then I can't even eat the thing; I'm so pissed off I have to throw it away. And I can't just gently toss it into the receptacle; oh no, I have to make a huge scene and slam-dunk it into the garbage can (which is made of wood, so the defective taco splats all over me and the carpet, making me even more irate), after which I choose to starve (and pout) and vow to never go there and attempt to order again!

6. Customer Service for mail order shopping

Can I just tell you that I HATE dealing with issues over the phone? I mean, truly, from the depths of my being, I despise the very vibration of the thought. There is nothing worse then having to solve a problem via telephone with someone in another time zone, who does not know you, does not really like you, does not care about your problem, and is just about to go on "break" (that is to say, if you are one of the lucky few that actually gets to talk to a real person at all).

First of all, it takes you about fifteen minutes just to get through the recorded spiel: "If you have a question about an order, press 1 (beep); if you have a question about an order that has been placed today, press 1; yesterday, press 2; three days ago, press 3."

With a sinking feeling, you realize your order was placed eleven days ago . . . (beep).

The "Voice" continues: "If your order that was placed eleven days ago has arrived, press 1; if the order that you placed eleven days ago has *not* arrived, press 2 (beep)." At this point, you're thinking you should be getting close to a live human connection (but you couldn't be more wrong). "If your order that you placed eleven days ago has not arrived and is *missing*, press 1; if your order that was placed eleven days ago that has not arrived needs to be re-routed, press 2 (beep); if your order—"

Why, all of a sudden, do you feel like you're trapped in a vintage children's book?—that one that mindlessly chants "I know an old lady who swallowed the shoe that squashed the spider that ate the bug that spooked the fly . . ."

Finally, you hear the sweet words you've longed for: "Please hold; your call will be answered in the order it was received." Thank you, God! (Wait a minute, where is my cheesy elevator music? Why am I not hearing any music? I better not have been disconnected, damn it.) You hear a series of clicks and then music (whew). You stay on the line for a few minutes, satisfied by this morsel of hope that—any minute now—you're going to be connected to a cheery operator.

Then the music stops (sweet), and again, you wait for the Voice. "Your call is very important to us. (Bull shit. If it was, you would pony up the extra cash and hire a few more warm bodies to field some of these calls.) "We are currently experiencing a high volume of calls." (Really? Maybe if your product shipped when it was supposed to, no one would have to take a half day off work to sit around on hold, waiting for someone to find the missing package!)

And still, the soulless Voice drones on: "And we are looking forward to servicing you soon. Your estimated wait time is . . . " (at this point you hold your breath) "approximately—" (What's this, a disclaimer? Why don't you take a page out of the Domino's Pizza play book and give me my shit free, if you don't answer my call in five minutes?) ". . . seventeen minutes."

WHAT?

At this point you weigh your options. First of all, you've already invested about nineteen minutes just getting to the moment where you are officially in line to be heard. Even though you want to hang up, it seems a little silly to let those minutes go in vain.

So, you decide to hold on. (But with each passing minute you're getting more and more upset, so you spend the entire "wait time" perfecting the snappy, sassy punch line you'll unleash on the agent—as soon as he or she finally decides to take your call. Something like "Well, I guess you guys are busy today, eh? Good thing I have nothing better to do!"

I think you get the picture as to where this is going. We've all been there. There are only a few possible outcomes to this scenario. Either your cellphone dies before your call gets answered, you can't hold your pee anymore (and, anyway, you're not on a cordless, so you have to either hang up or piss yourself), or you get that call you've been waiting for on the other line (at which point you bravely click over for a nanosecond to tell that person you'll call them right back—only to find that when you return to your "hold" line, all you can hear is the customer service hanging up the line because the actual, real-live agent thought no one was there). Of course, the most likely outcome is usually one of two things: Choice A, when the agent finally picks up your line, somehow you get disconnected, or, Choice B, when you get someone on the line, you feed them your whole sob story about your missing items (complete with snappy, sassy punch lines), and the agent regretfully tells you that she can't help you and will have to transfer you to another department.

And the cycle continues . . .

7. Krab with a "K" (Krab)

What exactly is *krab*, pray tell? Which food group would *krab* be representing anyway? Perhaps the same one as *cheez*? If you don't have access to crab, or you can't afford it, just go with the chicken, will you? (Incidentally, if you have to *pump* your cheez, I'm thinking it's a better choice just to skip the nachos, okay, amigo?)

8. Really small guys that drive really big jacked-up trucks

What is that, some kind of penis extension? You can see this huge truck barreling down the road equipped with the full-on naked lady mudguards, a thumping stereo, and a bumper sticker that says "Bringing Home the Bone." If you're lucky enough to see this thing park, you're expecting Paul-freaking-Bunyan to get out and go log some cedars, or something. But instead, you're puzzled by the five-foot-four gentleman that jumps out (and I do mean jumps, as it's a long way down) in a business suit and *Ray-Ban* shades. He has to throw all his weight into a single thrust to shut the door on this monster truck (and the handles are hitting him in the shoulder). It doesn't get any more pathetic than that.

9. Back hair

I'm sorry, guys, but if your woman tells you that she's attracted to your back hair, she's lying. Not too long ago, I was standing in line at the airport to go through security. As you know, those lines can be pretty long as the people weave back and forth, making their way to the metal detectors. There are plenty of people to watch, and there is plenty of time to do it. My sister and I were in line, and I spotted a guy about forty people behind us who was really hot. He had a great sense of style (expensive jeans, trendy sweater, cute little beanie hat) and dark, exotic hair. I pointed him out to my sister, and we spent a few minutes checking him out as we meandered through the line. At one point, his back ended up facing us, and I happened to glance in his direction. He was sporting the full-on "tuft," protruding from his trendy sweater! No shit, it was a total letdown. Here was this (otherwise) hot guy, and he had back hair brewing, like you read about. All I could think to myself was, *Poor guy, he'll never get laid.* It wasn't even tamed down at all. He might as well have put mousse in it and given it a name, because that thing was coming out to play!

So, if you're one of those men who is genetically prone to a generous dose of fur, do us all a favor and take it down to stubble, will you? No one wants to see it. You won't find a lady that likes to brush it (just get it lasered, or something). If nothing else, wear a turtleneck already!

10. When my husband gets sick

Why is it that whenever men get sick, all of a sudden they expect the world to stop? I mean, they expect their wives (girlfriends, significant others and, I would bet, even booty calls) to drop everything and cater to their every need. No shit, my husband, though I love him dearly, practically retreats to infancy every time he battles a cough (a green lugi, heaven forbid, would put him out for at least two weeks).

News flash! Women get sick all the time; most men don't notice this because we still have to go to work, take care of the kids, pay the bills, drive the carpool, hit the grocery store, make dinner, give the baths, and pet the dog. Slowing down to take it easy is not an option for today's woman. She could be spewing blood and have a nail lodged in her leg and still have to drop the kids at school (and pick up the dry cleaning) before she could even consider driving (herself) to the hospital. A guy, on the other hand, gets a sniffle and he's whining and moaning like he's about to implode. He has everyone in the house feeling sorry for him, catering to his every whim, while he lays in bed (all day) with some Häagen-Dazs, ringing a damn bell for you so that you'll come change the channel for him! A headache? Well a headache would send him over the edge to the point that he's wondering if he'll ever be able to work again—because the throbbing is *just so bad* that you could never understand the pain he's enduring. Puh-leeze! (I'm pretty sure the part I will never understand is why he's making such a big deal out of it, the big wimp!)

I can remember a time when I was working for Nordstrom and I came down with food poisoning. (For those of you who have experienced that, you know how bad that sucks!) The thought of staying home from work did not even cross my mind. I was more concerned with how I was going to make it through my forty-five-minute commute without having to barf or shitting myself. It happened to be the night that we were doing the end of the year inventory, and I had a whole section that I was in charge of. If I wasn't there, that section would be assigned to someone else. How could I ever be considered for a future promotion if word got out that I didn't complete my section? I would be letting the rest of my co-workers down, and they would hate me. My department manager would be so disappointed in me that every time she saw me she'd secretly wonder if I was really sick, or if I was just faking it—to get out of doing the undesirable task of ticket counting. Then my store manager (who did not even know my real name) would look at me in disgust and know me only as the blonde Inventory Dodger from the second floor. Needless to say, there was no way that I was going to skip inventory. That is not the way that we women roll, right ladies? (Okay, off my soapbox. I feel a stress headache coming on.)

11. (Okay, I lied; my Top Ten just multiplied.) Last but not least . . . people who walk around with whiteheads they don't take care of

If I'm, say, standing in line at Barnes and Noble, I might begin talking to the dude in line, just in front of me. Then I quickly discover he has a big, juicy whitehead on his face. At this point, I can no longer concentrate on what he is saying. He might as well shut up because I'm not hearing a word. All I'm thinking about is how I can possibly finagle a way to politely offer to pop the shit out of that boil on his nose. It doesn't even have to be that big; I can spot the baby ones sprouting, and they're just as delicious. A zit doesn't have to have its own heartbeat in order to get my attention; I will happily take them down in all sizes. For some reason I have a sick obsession with popping other people's zits (ask my husband's back), and I get a twisted sense of accomplishment from the particularly plump ones (come to find out, not everyone would count this as one of my more alluring qualities). If you don't want me to pop it for you (I understand we haven't even been formally introduced yet), fine. But for the love of God, take care of that shit yourself before you go out in public.

The Rental

In a world . . . (eerie movie-trailer voice) *where Sarah and Brian make rash, quick, and subsequently regrettable decisions, they once came upon a house for sale that would change life as they knew it.* (Oh no, there was nothing wrong with their current house; in fact, it was brand new. But this one was older, smaller, more expensive, and needed lots of maintenance.) *So Sarah and Brian* (on a whim) *decided to put their house on the market and buy the other* (project). *Sarah, every bit the princess, could not actually live in the new home until some basic renovations were made, so they needed to come up with an alternative living arrangement quickly. Sarah's idea was to purchase a condo a few miles away. But Brian was way too practical for that. According to his calculations, there was nothing rational about having three mortgages. Instead, Brian's solution was to purchase a 32-foot Air*

Stream and live on the new property during the renovation; then they could put the RV to good use as a family for years to come—after they were living comfortably in their new home. Sarah was quick to stamp "Veto" on that plan. She was not about to embark on a three-month camping trip with two kids in a 250-square-foot, rolling metal asylum. Then, as they drove down the road on the way to their new house, one day they saw the answer to their problems. It was bright blue and stood on the side of the road like a beacon of light. It was . . . The Rental.

When I pulled up to the house I immediately knew it would be perfect, even before I went inside. It was, after all, less than a half mile from our new house. It was right on the water (well, across the street from the water, but there was no house on the other side of the road, so it was just as good as waterfront). It was small, had a huge detached garage, and it was close to school, shopping, and other local attractions.I met the landlord for a quick look-see, but as far as I was concerned, it was all a formality: I was going to be moving in. As long as a rat did not run across my toe when I walked in, then I was going to call this place home for the next ninety days! It was nice: small, but clean. It had two bedrooms, one bath, and a small kitchen and living area. It would be a big change after our 4,500-square-foot home, but again, it was only for a few weeks, and it would be fun. It would be like a big slumber party for the kids, and Brian and I could pretend we were living in a college dorm for the summer.

"I'll take it," I said.

Let's fast forward to moving day. As you can imagine, most of our belongings were not going to fit into The Rental. So, everything from our garage went straight into the storage unit, which we were renting up the street. Truth be told, this was fine with me, because this meant that I did not have to move things twice (well, I should say, *Brian* did not have to move things twice). Our furniture and such was all being moved into the basement of the new house. We were doing most of the remodel on the main level of the house, so the basement would be a safe place for our furniture and valuable items during this whole process of upheaval.

Being the minimalist that I am (did I just say that out loud?), I made the brilliant decision that we would throw a mattress on the floor for the kids to share in one room, and another for Brian and I in the larger bedroom. Once the mattresses were down, I quickly realized there was not much room for anything else. In the kids' room, I backed the queen size mattress up so it was touching walls on *three* sides, which left about three feet of space on one side for the kids to walk, get dressed, and house all their other worldly possessions. My solution to this was to give each child exactly *one* laundry basket to put their clothes in, and *one* laundry basket to put everything else they owned in. Then, the baskets were stacked on top of each other. The rule was: *everything* had to remain in the basket *at all times* (you can see this is going to go downhill quickly).

In our bedroom we had the mattress at one end of the room, and a stand with a TV on it at the other. There were two closets (bonus) at the far end of the room, and each had a set of sliding doors. We immediately took the doors off to create the illusion that the room was bigger (and, for what it's worth, I think it worked). I knew we were in trouble after I was done loading my clothes into the closet. Once I got a chance to stand back and admire the fact that I had somehow managed to cram most of them into the confined space provided, I noticed that the closet rod was not only bowing in the middle, but the cross-bar (which was supporting the rod) was actually digging into the drywall, slowly creating a hole under the weight of my garments. (Oops! I guess this is why renters have to put down damage deposits, huh?)

Another one of my more inspired ideas: I decided to forgo using our couch in The Rental and bring in the treadmill instead. My thought process was that since it was only temporary anyway (and we obviously did not have space for both), I would be better off having a treadmill in the living room, instead of a couch. That way, when and if I found myself watching TV, I would at least be exercising, instead of wasting away on the sofa getting fat (it made total sense at the time). So, at my direction, the couch went to the basement at the remodel, and the treadmill came to The Rental.

The rest of the furniture consisted of one of the small patio tables from our deck at the old house (which would now serve as our dining room table), two stuffed children's chairs from Pottery Barn Kids, and an end table made out of a NASCAR tire. ("Oh, but you don't understand, Sarah; it's a real, *authentic* Daytona racing tire, and NASCAR fans would kill to have this table!" To which I say, let's put it on eBay, then, and make someone's dreams come true!) There was also a little metal cart that we used for our computer printer (if, that is, your budget won't allow for anything over twenty bucks for that little line item).

Welcome home. We were going to love it here.

At first the kids were really excited. The idea of sharing a room was thrilling to them. I think it felt like an all-access pass to stay up late talking, or sneak toys into the bed, or something. Plus, they felt pretty good about the fact that no matter where Mom and Dad were in the house, they would be able to see us, literally. Brian and I were excited, too. Our stay would only be for a few months (at most), and with all the excitement of the remodel to distract us, time would fly by. Also, it was going to be especially easy on me.

The major downsize in square footage meant that I had virtually nothing to clean, a bonus in itself. Couple that with the fact that (as I soon found out) the oven in the new digs did not work (the angels were watching over me), and the small fridge only held a fraction of the food needed to properly nourish a family of four, AND there was no dishwasher on the premises (is that even up to code?), we had the makings for one happy Mommy. All I knew was that even though that refrigerator was leaning at a slight angle (perhaps because the floor in the kitchen was anything but level) it did serve its purpose by providing the consistent resting place for our book of choice, that proverbial menu . . . the phone book. It would be take-out for the Nilsen's, and I would not hear another word about it.

The floor plan of our new house would take some getting use to as well. There would be no more privacy for Mom and Dad. The whole house capped out at about 600 square feet, and if you stood in any given spot, you could see (and of course hear) wall-to-wall in this joint. My favorite nuance was this: when you walked from the living room toward the bathroom the floor, the joists gave rise to at least a fifteen percent grade (even though it was only about six steps from one room to the next, you still felt like you were tripping on acid). Thus our bathroom door did not open and close freely, what with the tight squeeze of the uneven floor; in fact, it never even approached the completely closed (and locked) position. This little irritation became increasingly important when someone was *in* the bathroom, because the light for the bathroom was wired directly to the fan. This might not seem to be that big of a deal—except the fan resembled something more like a jet engine than the normal bathroom variety. So every time the bathroom light went on, the whole house would shake (or so it seemed) with the loud roaring of a fan that could blow the stink off a shit. So it was either pee in the dark (which is not a good choice for a four-year-old boy, trust me), or whoever was in the living room would just have to learn to turn the TV up a few notches when someone went into the restroom, and then turn the TV down again when the light went off. We could adapt. Things could be worse (so I thought).

Another concern I found with the bathroom door not shutting all the way was that The Rental was situated right on the curb of a very busy street. On the morning of my first shower, I got out of the stall and stepped right out of the bathroom. Lo and behold, I was now in the living room, about twenty feet away from one of the busiest roads in the county. For a minute I just stood there, transfixed, watching the cars fly by from the front window, and I swear I saw my ex-boyfriend drive by (good thing I'd shaved). And, in case you are wondering, the answer is YES. I was standing there *completely nude.* There was nowhere to hide. To do so, I had to leave the bathroom, and to get from point A to point B, I had to travel via the living room, which was like a big fish bowl, of sorts, a small space with a *very* large window (who designed this house anyway, Dr. Seuss?) facing the known world. Everyone could see in as they drove along the scenic road in front. Note to self: next time bring robe into bathroom. (Another note to self: purchase robe.)

You see, at my previous home we never had to worry about walking around the house naked; neighbors couldn't see in our windows because our house was nestled high above the hills. The Rental, on the other hand, was practically using the sidewalk curb for its foundation. From that day on, even though the little house had an amazing view of the water, the curtains would be drawn at all times, and we would get our weather forecast from the news anchor like the rest of society (no more looking to the north and trying to use the sun and cloud patterns). So much for the "view" being worth the cost of admission, eh?

I can still remember waking up in the morning after our first night in The Rental. Or a better phrase for it might be, *being woken up*. I must have been in a major state of R.E.M., or something, because I can remember being semi-unconscious and hearing a loud thundering sound. I jumped up immediately, thinking we were having an earthquake. Then, I did what any concerned mother would do. I crawled back into bed and yelled out to the kids. (Oh, come on, they weren't *that* far away. Remember, it was all of fifteen feet; they could hear me.)

False alarm! It was not an earthquake, or any other natural disaster, for that matter. It was actually the sound of my husband hitting his razor against the porcelain sink in the adjacent bathroom as he was shaving. The freaking walls at *Casa* Nilsen were so paper-thin that the noise (and don't forget that fan mimicking the Amtrak) not only woke me from a restful slumber, it also tricked my whole body into thinking we were in the midst of a national emergency. We were going to have to take a closer look at how this whole morning ritual was going to go down—if we had any chance of sticking it out in *Le Rental* for any extended period of time (because if Mama don't get her sleep, ain't nobody happy).

Nighttimes were, perhaps, the most memorable times of all. In typical households (or so I have read) the evening hours are the time when families hunker down by the fire after a warm meal and either watch a movie, curled up together on the couch, or maybe play a board game. But not if you are a family living in total disarray in elf-sized spaces, suffering a scarcity of personal effects and the complete lack of . . . *heat!*

Now, before you go and break out your genius on me, yes, the heat was on. As a matter of fact, to any passersby, our chimney was a'blowin' at The Rental. I always knew that the heat was on because the fan (much like the bathroom fan) was so freakin' loud that it made normal conversation impossible in the general living space of the house. The heater would kick on, grumble at an insane decibel for about ten minutes, and then shut off. Just when your ears stopped ringing, it would fire up again. The interesting thing was, however, that the house never seemed to warm up much beyond fifty degrees. Remember that I told you the place was not exactly a palace, so it should not have taken much gas to heat up this shoebox, right? Even though I thought I would use the treadmill (and the body heat generated from a good workout) to keep me warm, my ass was typically camped out on the kid's foam Pottery Barn chairs, about ten millimeters off the frozen floor. I had to get up and walk around the kitchen during commercials, because if I sat for more than about fifteen minutes, my ass would literally ice over. For the longest time I could not figure out why the temperature always felt subarctic in the house since the heater was continuously running. Then one day I figured it out. During a conversation with the landlord, he *happened* to mention that there was no insulation in the crawlspace under the house (or in any of the exterior walls, for that matter). Nice! So all our efforts to heat the place were, literally, going out the window. I could see this being even more of a problem in the winter (good thing we would only be there for a few short months). *Yeah, right!*

If you have ever gone through a remodel (and lived to tell about it), then you know that it never goes as planned. The ninety-day project morphed into the ten-month project (from hell). Oh yes, our little remodel turned into a major teardown, and we basically started over from the foundation. So not only did we spend the following winter at The Rental (by the way, the heater did give out, probably from working overtime, and we went from having the deafening furnace running non-stop to icicles forming on our noses, while we slept on in silence), but we spent the better part of the whole year there, as well.

It was a Merry Christmas at The Rental. There was no room for a tree of course, and, silly me, I thought this was actually a good thing. I was going to "get out of" having to decorate for once. But a few days before the big event my son looked up at me with concern and reminded me that we'd *almost forgotten* to put up our tree. So we had to put a two-foot faux tree on top of the tire table in the living room (displacing, of course, the miscellaneous papers and candles already occupying that prime real estate.) There was no room for gifts. The kids' laundry baskets were plumb full of trinkets, so all their new toys would have to take up residence out in the back of my car for the next (several) months until the new house was completed. (I volunteered Brian to be captain of the team that would break that news to the kids.)

You don't have to be Socrates to figure out that there was not an Easter Egg hunt at the Nilsen's that year. No sign of merriment and no plastic grass for us.

One by one, the holidays passed us by.

Happy freakin' Fourth of July, folks. We owned a beautiful waterfront home about 500 yards from The Rental, but we wouldn't be hosting a BBQ. I'd even purchased some cute little invitations for the housewarming party, in hopes that we'd be settled in time for the big Independence Day celebration, but it didn't happen. Instead, we sat in the (cold, dark) Rental and pouted, while the sounds of gassed-up Sea-Doos and the giggles of water skiers filled the bay, only steps from The Rental door. The sun was shining brightly through the shades of the front window, and we could see shadows of our friends playing on the water and enjoying the festivities. But we were so pissed off that we were still stuck in the shoe box that we refused to partake.

Come September (kids, gather 'round; I want to take your "first day of school pictures" in front of the treadmill), we were *finally* ready to move. Can I get an Amen?

I had managed to parlay ten months of take-out food into fifteen pounds of regret—right on my hips. The treadmill, which was supposed to serve as motivation for me to stay in shape, was nothing more than a place for me to throw extra coats and blankets (God knows we needed them).

The kids' laundry baskets with their clothes and toys were nothing but a mound of confusion, and their shared mattress was more of a landing pad for everything else they owned that did not have an appropriate space.

Over time, the contents of my closet somehow oozed out, spilling into the bedroom. There were cardboard boxes (that I had never unpacked from the move) now serving as makeshift "drawers" (in some kind of phantom dresser that only I could see, I guess) with shirts and pants draped all over them, as if they were *supposed* to be there.

The small patio table that was supposed to be used for our dining purposes in the kitchen area was constantly littered with papers, trinkets, and other random things (but, I am sure, very important things—had I been able to get visual confirmation). So if we actually wanted to *eat* at the table, we would have to spend fifteen minutes clearing it off first. This posed a new problem: where to move the stuff once we cleared it from the table. There simply were no other choices; all other countertops, tabletops, mattresses, TV tops and treadmills were spoken for. The only feasible solution was to leave the clutter, jump in the car, and take the family to IHOP, chalking it up to another day down, another day closer to getting the hell out of The Rental.

Those ten months might possibly have been the longest ten months of my life. Every day we'd go down to the new house and stare longingly at the progress and contemplate exactly how much progress we'd really need see in order to move in (after all, The Rental did not have heat or food, so all we really needed was running water, and even that was pretty much an even toss).

But one thing is certain, once we did move in, we sure did appreciate our new home. Now, there's not a day that goes by that we don't take a moment to count our blessings. Every time I turn on the bathroom light and the fan does not blow me backwards, I think of The Rental. Every time I sit on the living room floor and ice crystals don't form on my ass, I think about The Rental. Every time I tuck my kids into their (separate) beds and kiss them good night (separately), I think about The Rental. And every time I walk around my house naked after a shower (or sometimes just for the heck of it), I thank God that I'm no longer living in The Rental. Yes, it is true, that which doesn't kill us makes us stronger. (You might be thinking this is a little dramatic, folks, but trust me... there were times.)

I drove by that little blue house the other day, and there was again a sign outside that read "For Rent." A young couple had stopped outside in the driveway, and they were pulling a flyer out of the information box just as we passed. For a minute I almost got nostalgic thinking, *It was not really that bad.* Just then, a little voice belonging to my five-year-old son piped up from the back seat: "Mom, roll your window down so we can warn them!"

First, I'd Like to Thank the Academy...

This is where I get to let all the people in my life that are important to me know it (and I sure hope I don't forget anyone...that would be bad as it will be captured in print for generations to come.)

First and foremost I want to thank my husband Brian. During the crafting of this book there were many nights I was up at my computer (late) and I know you were wishing that I would just come to bed already. But instead of complaining, you'd allow me to hover over my keyboard and continue to work on my passion. I always love and respect you, and treasure the fact that you love and respect me enough to let me chase my dreams (no matter how crazy they might seem at times.)

I also want to thank my sister, and life long best friend Jeni Zapatka. Without you...there would be no book. After each chapter you were the one that I'd send it to for honest feedback *(so I guess, if this book if this book is a flop, it is your fault ha!)* My whole life you've been my biggest cheerleader, and I have learned a lot from watching you become a success in your own life. You're amazing.

I want to thank my sister-in-law Joan. By me baring my own dirty laundry in this book...I sometimes threw you under the bus with me. Thanks for being so real. I treasure our relationship and I know that God put us together for a greater purpose.

Thanks to my mom who still loves me even though I "outted" her to the whole world that she bought her bras from a box...

To my Dad who raised me to believe in myself, to be honest and not to take myself too seriously...which is the essence of this whole book.

To my beautiful children Kennedy and Carter who had to be quiet and let Mommy work at times when they would rather "not"...I am so proud of who you are both becoming.

And to the rest of my friends and family who supported me through out the rest of this process...especially the ones who allowed me to use your name and stories in this book. I appreciate you allowing me be real.

Thank you to the wonderful and talented Amy Zundel for your amazing design of my book cover. I am so blessed to call you friend; and I so appreciate you taking the time to do this for me. You're such a gift.

Thank you to the talented Ms. Amanda Ford and Deanna Davis for taking the time to mentor me during the process of this book.

It meant a lot that you both spent time with me...I appreciate it very much.

Thank you to Angie Shields who sweetly wrote my *very first* book review: "I'm glad it doesn't suck so that I won't have to lie when I recommend it to my friends"

To Supra herself, Suzie Kerr, who not only shares my dreams, but believes that we will accomplish them...I see our name in lights someday, girl!

A big thank you to America's Dream Coach Marcia Wieder for teaching me how to Dream Big in the first place.

And of course my coach, Kerri Yates, for hearing me but refusing to allowing me to listen to my gremlins.

Last but not least, my amazing editor Laurie Klein. You took a leap of faith taking on this project and helped me immensely. Your wisdom will help me far beyond this book.

And to all of my Sensaria Sisters who read my chapters before the book was published and gave me so much support and encouragement...YOU guys are the ones who gave me the strength and the courage to move forward when at times I wondered if I could do it. YOU were the faces that I pictured standing in line at Barnes and Noble ordering copies of this book...(so don't let me down now)

One thing is for sure, I had so much fun with this book that I know you ain't heard the last from me!

God Bless you all!

About the Author

Although writing has always been a passion of hers, this is Sarah's first book. When she isn't working she loves to shop for the perfect shoes and travel in search sunny beaches. This should come as no surprise seeing as Sarah was born and raised near Seattle, Washington where she still lives with her two children, Kennedy and Carter and her wonderful husband, Brian.

Printed in the United States
88878LV00004B/238-273/A